A Contemplative Rosary:
Praying the Mysteries
with Scripture, Song & Icons

Bob Hurd
MUSIC

Elaine Park
BIBLICAL REFLECTIONS

Charles Rohrbacher
ICONOGRAPHY

WITH A FOREWORD BY
Most Reverend Michael W. Warfel
BISHOP OF JUNEAU, ALASKA

A Contemplative Rosary: Praying the Mysteries with Scripture, Song & Icons
ISBN 1-57992-128-0

OCP Publications
5536 NE Hassalo
Portland, OR 97213
Phone 1-800-LITURGY (548-8749)
E-mail: liturgy@ocp.org
ocp.org

Publisher: John J. Limb
Editorial Processes Director: Vic Cozzoli
Manager of Liturgical Resources: Paulette McCoy
Managing Editor: Eric Schumock
Project Editor: Bari Colombari; Editorial assistance: Michael R. Prendergast

Senior Designer: Patricia Burraston
Art Director: Jean Germano
Iconographer: Charles Rohrbacher

Printed in Mexico.

A Contemplative Rosary: Praying the Mysteries with Scripture, Song & Icons:
People's Book . . . . edition 12726
Leader's Guide (with accompaniments) . . edition 12727
CD, The Luminous Mysteries . . . . edition 12728
CD ROM (Icons) . . . . edition 12729

Table of Contents

Rosary of the Blessed Virgin Mary   1
    Bishop Michael W. Warfel

Incarnation and Icon   5
    Charles Rohrbacher

A Contemplative Rosary   7
    Bob Hurd

Mary, the Dawn   11
Pilgrim Prayer   12
The Rosary (Opening)   13

The Joyful Mysteries
    The Annunciation   14
    The Visitation   18
    The Nativity of Jesus   22
    The Presentation   26
    The Finding of Jesus in the Temple   30

The Luminous Mysteries
    The Baptism of Jesus   34
    The Wedding Feast at Cana   38
    The Proclamation of the Kingdom of God   42
    The Transfiguration   46
    Christ's Institution of the Eucharist   50

The Sorrowful Mysteries
    The Agony in the Garden   54
    The Scourging at the Pillar   58
    The Crowning with Thorns   62
    The Carrying of the Cross   66
    The Crucifixion   70

The Glorious Mysteries
    The Resurrection   74
    The Ascension   78
    The Descent of the Holy Spirit   82
    The Assumption   86
    The Coronation   90

Salve Regina   94
Concluding Dialogue and Prayer   94
Let It Be Done to Us   96
Bibliography   98

Rosary of the Blessed Virgin Mary

On October 16, 2002, Pope John Paul II issued his Apostolic Letter to the Church, *Rosarium Virginis Mariae* (Rosary of the Virgin Mary) that dedicated a full year to promotion of the Rosary. The Pope proposed his Apostolic Letter as a Marian accompaniment to *Novo Millennio Ineunte* (Entering the New Millennium), an earlier Apostolic Letter as the Church entered a third millennium of life.

In his Apostolic Letter on the Rosary, the Holy Father called on the people of God to rediscover the depth and richness of the Rosary as a form of contemplative prayer. In *Novo Millennio Ineunte*, he stressed the urgency for Christian communities to discover and learn from "genuine schools of prayer" in a world so filled with violence and war. (*NMI*, #33) In *Rosarium Virginis Mariae*, he wrote,

> At the start of a millennium which began with the terrifying attacks of 11 September 2001, a millennium that witnesses every day in numerous parts of the world fresh scenes of bloodshed and violence, to rediscover the Rosary means to immerse oneself in contemplation of the mystery of Christ who 'is our peace', since he made 'the two of us one, and broke down the dividing wall of hostility' (Ephesians 2:14). Consequently, one cannot recite the Rosary without feeling caught up in a clear commitment to advancing peace…(*RVM, # 6*).

The Holy Father also asked for believers to rediscover the Rosary as a genuine form of prayer in order to counter what he termed "a certain crisis of the Rosary." (*RVM*, #4) He feared that contemporary trends as well as the theological and liturgical milieu of this age were diminishing the Rosary as a valid form of prayer in the minds of many Christians. By reclaiming the Rosary he hoped that the faithful would understand it as a form of personal prayer, an aid to spiritual formation and an instrument of evangelization.

In response to the Holy Father's concerns, the Diocese of Juneau organized a pilgrimage that was celebrated during the week of the Feast of Our Lady of the Rosary, October 7, 2003. The pilgrimage provided an opportunity to promote the Rosary not only as a contemporary way to pray but a timeless form of prayer. For the pilgrimage, an icon entitled Our Lady of the Rosary was commissioned and written by Charles Rohrbacher of Juneau, Alaska. The icon included the five additional Mysteries of Light (Luminous Mysteries) that had been proposed by Pope John Paul II. (*RVM*, #21) The icon was used as a focus for the pilgrimage since the Pope's Apostolic Letter had suggested the use of iconography to portray the mysteries. In addition, a musical setting of the Rosary interspersed with appropriate passages of Scripture was commissioned and composed by Bob Hurd of San Jose, California. This musical setting was a highlight for the pilgrimage weekend as pilgrims from throughout the Diocese assembled at the Parish of Saint Paul in Juneau. They contemplated the Mysteries of Light and sang the musical setting of the Rosary before the icon of Our Lady of the Rosary. Other highlights during the pilgrimage were two morning conferences to connect the Rosary to the Scriptures with Dr. Elaine Park, Dean of Studies at Oregon's Mount Angel Seminary providing this biblically-based catechesis on Mary.

An Instrument for Contemplating the Paschal Mystery

Rather than detract from the church's liturgy, the prayer of the Rosary can introduce, echo and support the church's communal prayer. The Rosary of the Blessed Virgin Mary is an instrument for contemplating the Paschal Mystery. Emphasizing significant moments in the life of Christ, the mysteries help those who pray the Rosary to "…contemplate with Mary the face of Christ" (*RVM*, #3). Beginning with the mystery of the Annunciation, each mystery issues a call to the believer to embody salvation in Christ. In other words, contemplation upon the mysteries of the Rosary involves more than recollection of what occurred in history with Mary and Jesus. The mysteries of the Rosary are not mere history lessons but profound calls of faith. The expectation and hope is that those who pray the Rosary and contemplate its mysteries will immerse themselves in the life of Christ.

The Rosary is meant to be contemplative prayer that both venerates the Blessed Virgin Mary and offers a devotional way to worship God. As a contemplative form of prayer, the hope is that those who pray it will desire to grow closer to God. It is expected that those who truly contemplate its mysteries will be led to grow spiritually and to respond more deeply to the call of God in their lives.

The scene of the Annunciation—the first mystery announced—establishes an underlying theme for all the ensuing mysteries of the Rosary. In the conversation between the Archangel Gabriel and the young Jewish woman of faith, the announcement of God's favor is proclaimed. An unspoken reality behind the words of the Archangel's proclamation is the need for Mary freely to consent in faith to the will of God. Her invitation and call to do God's will is the invitation and call presented to Christians of every age who must consent freely in faith to the will of God in their lives. The consent of the young Mary to bear the Son of God in her womb is a significant aspect of the mystery. Her acceptance to the Archangel's announcement becomes a model for every Christian. As Pope John Paul II wrote in *Rosarium Virginis Mariae*:

> If it is the Father's plan to unite all things in Christ (cf. Ephesians 1:10), then the whole of the universe is in some way touched by the divine favor with which the Father looks upon Mary and makes her the Mother of his Son. The whole of humanity, in turn, is embraced by the fiat with which she readily agrees to the will of God. (*RVM*, #20)

Call, Mystery and Mysticism

As a contemplative form of prayer based upon various elements of the Paschal Mystery, the prayer of the Rosary involves call, mystery, and mysticism. It is a basic belief of Christian faith that all are called by God to share life in the communion of saints. Life in Christ is the meaning and purpose of human existence. The reason Jesus was born and died on a cross was to redeem a fallen humanity and bring salvation to anyone who would turn to him. Those throughout salvation history who have heard and responded to the call of Christ proclaim with Prophet Simeon,

> "…for my eyes have seen your salvation,
>> which you prepared in sight of all the peoples,
>> a light for revelation to the Gentiles,
>> and glory for your people Israel." (Luke 2:30–32)

A call refers to an individual's vocation in life and is filled with divine mystery. As distinct from an occupation—though an occupation may be interwoven with vocation—a vocation involves a divine reality. A vocation is specifically concerned with life in Christ and is celebrated through baptism. The vocation all Christians share is baptism. A call from God, however, must be lived out concretely. For each person, the call is unique. No one experiences the exact same context in life, lives in the same time and space, has the same circumstances in life or shares the same physical or psychological traits that makes them who they are. Each individual, within her or his own time and place in history and with all that makes them unique, is invited to respond to a call to live in Christ. Each individual who responds to this call must do so within their unique circumstances and context in life and with the character traits, qualities, abilities, and resources with which God has blessed them.

For some, the call of God is clearly heard and comes early in life. For others, it is perceived gradually and may come late in life, often requiring attentive listening. Once heard, it requires even more attention lest they lose sight of the call and not remain faithful to it. A call is never just a one time event but an ongoing reality; likewise, neither is the response to the call a one-time event. The dynamic involved is more like an ongoing conversation with God that must continue throughout life. Occasions of a calling vary widely. While they may be perceived in moments filled with noise and in the midst of a crowd, more likely they are heard during times of quiet and solitude, and almost certainly during prayer. In every case, they must be sustained through prayer. An essential dynamic involved is attending to the voice of the Caller and responding in faith.

To respond to a call from God is to encounter divine mystery. The term mystery, as used in the mysteries of the Rosary, is not always clearly understood. For some, mystery refers to a concept that is impenetrable and beyond comprehension. Because God is infinite and humans are finite, they are to accept the propositions of faith without question. Others may view mystery as a puzzle to be solved. All one need do is place the pieces of a puzzle together in the proper order and all will become crystal clear and the riddle will be solved. Understandings of this sort get in the way of truly appreciating the mysteries of faith as presented through events in the life of Christ. People who approach mystery as a call of faith to be embraced and lived-out see a deeper reality than that which is impenetrable or merely a riddle to be unraveled.

Mystery signifies an encounter with the divine. Human beings, finite and fixed in history, can only partially understand an infinite and eternal God. This is not to say that human beings can know but little about God—only that they can never plumb the depths of divine reality. In actuality, people can and do understand much about what God has revealed to humanity. Through contemplation on what God has revealed (i.e., mysteries of faith), Christians grow in their knowledge of God as well as in their relationship with God in Christ. They also discover, at an increasingly deeper level, the unique person that God has called them to be in Christ, i.e., an individual who is fully alive in Christ.

To embody divine mystery is to embrace mysticism, another concept not well understood by many. And yet, mysticism is an important element for fruitful contemplation on the mysteries of faith. Mysticism refers to the relationship to which all the baptized are called. While commonly relegated solely to figures such as Saint Teresa of

Avila, Saint John of the Cross or Saint Ignatius of Loyola, mysticism actually pertains to every disciple of the Lord. Individuals baptized into Christ need to recall that, by virtue of their baptism, they are incorporated into the mystical body of Christ. By virtue of baptism into Christ, all are called to mysticism. Mysticism applies not solely to those people of faith who have had sublime experiences of the presence of Christ or whose lives were so extraordinarily holy and who are now recalled in the canon of saints. Nor does mysticism refer solely to those who have had ecstatic experiences of the presence of God in their lives. Mysticism is for every Christian. Holiness can and must be sought by each Christian. After all, the purpose and meaning of human existence is to become a saint. This occurs as people respond to the God, who is always and everywhere available through the Spirit of Jesus.

While a number of select holy women and men in history are renowned for their heroic and exemplary witness, they are the exception. Most people discover holiness in relatively unexceptional circumstances. The extent to which their lives become known as holy is known only by a few. Striving for holiness does not really include the desire to be known in history as a member listed in the canon of saints. It involves rather, a desire to lose oneself in Christ and to be immersed in the paschal mystery. A person becomes holy by being open to the grace of God at work in her or his life. It is through such openness to the availability of the Spirit that a person becomes a mystic. Christians, who respond to the grace of God within the circumstances of their own time and place in history as best and as fully as they can, truly become holy people. Whether they are ever listed officially in the canon of saints is irrelevant. Such openness leads individuals to become all that they can be in Christ and, as such, mystics. It is to this kind of mystical experience—that of being fully alive in Christ—that all Christians are called. In essence, this is exactly what the mysteries of the Rosary propose. They are examples of faith-filled response to the call of God within particular circumstances and in a particular time and place in the history of salvation. To contemplate them is to attend to the call to embody the mystery.

Contemplation on the mysteries of the Rosary provides a means to assist a believer to grow spiritually. When prayed faithfully, devoutly and truly as contemplative prayer, they lead those who contemplate them into the midst of the paschal mystery.

—Most Rev. Michael W. Warfel
Bishop of the Diocese of Juneau, Alaska
Summer 2004

Incarnation and Icon

In his Apostolic Letter *Rosarium Virginis Mariae* the Holy Father urged Catholics to rediscover the Rosary (or if unacquainted with this form of prayer, to encounter it for the first time.) He spoke of the Rosary as a prayer that while being clearly Marian in character, is fundamentally focused on the person of Christ and contains within it the "depth of the Gospel message in its entirety." The Holy Father stressed the contemplative character of the Rosary, the recitation of which invites meditation on the mysteries of the life of Jesus. He noted, too, that the Rosary, while not a substitute for *lectio divina* (the traditional method of reading, meditating on, praying with and contemplating the Word of God), presupposes and supports the practice of *lectio.*

What particularly stood out in the letter was section 29: "Announcing Each Mystery." The Holy Father wrote:

> Announcing each mystery, and perhaps even using a suitable icon to portray it, is as it were *to open up a scenario* on which to focus our attention. The words direct the imagination and the mind towards a particular episode or moment in the life of Christ. In the Church's traditional spirituality, the veneration of icons and the many devotions appealing to the senses, as well as the method of prayer proposed by St.Ignatius of Loyola in the Spiritual Exercises, make use of visual and imaginative elements (the *compositio loci*), judged to be of great help in concentrating the mind on the particular mystery. This is a methodology, moreover, which *corresponds to the inner logic of the Incarnation*: in Jesus, God wanted to take on human features. It is through his bodily reality that we are led into contact with the mystery of his divinity.

Note that the Holy Father specifically recommends the employment of icons (as opposed to proposing the use of religious art in general) and mentions the veneration of icons as the first of a number of ways traditional Christian spirituality has visually contemplated the mystery of the Incarnation. He goes on to underline that this use of images corresponds to the inner of logic of the Incarnation itself, in which the Word became flesh and through which human beings are brought into communion with Jesus and through him, with the life-giving Triune God.

The Holy Father's proposal to incorporate the icon into the practice of the Rosary is an invitation to a deeper understanding of the icon itself. Icon is a Greek word that means image. In the creation account (Genesis 1:26) the human being is made in the image of God (*icon* in the Greek translation of the original Hebrew text). Although human beings are made in the divine image by God, the Old Testament absolutely forbids the people of Israel themselves from making images of God. This prohibition (which rejected all representations of the human person) was intended to safeguard the radical otherness and transcendence of God in a cultural and religious environment that endowed images of deities with spiritual power. From the perspective of the Old Covenant, any attempt to make an image of the God of Israel was condemned as an act of idolatry, which confused the vain imaginings of the human mind for the living God.

However, with the Incarnation, all this changes. In the person of Jesus can be found the perfect image of God. Although Saint John the Evangelist does not use the word 'icon,' he speaks of Christ as the one in whom the Father has become visible

(John 1:14; 12:45;14:9). Saint Paul describes Jesus as the icon (or image) of the invisible God (Colossians 1:15) and teaches us that believers, by their baptism and transformation in Christ, exchange their old nature, darkened and distorted by sin, for the new nature in Christ, "which is being renewed, for knowledge, in the image of its creator" (Colossians 3:10).

The invisible God, who in the Old Testament could not be imagined or depicted, dwelt among us in Jesus, the perfect image of God, uniting in his person the divine nature and the human nature. And because Jesus possesses a complete and full human nature, and since the fullness of God is revealed to us in the person of Jesus, the God-Man, his image (or icon) is the true and reliable image of God.

It should be noted that the first or proto-icon of Jesus is that of the Holy Face, received, according to holy tradition, directly from the Lord himself. Like the sacred scriptures, there is a canon of iconography, that is to say, those images recognized by the church as inspired and proposed to the faithful as the word of God and a source of revealed doctrine. Religious paintings are the personal faith expression of their creators, which is why artists such as Fra Angelico, Michaelangelo, Dürer, Raphael, El Greco, Rubens, Roualt, and Chagall painted often-times identical religious themes in such different (and even antithetical ways.) By way of contrast, the icon, while always a new interpretation, presents not the subjective vision of the icon painter, but the objective faith of the entire church. Thus, icon painters strive to adhere strictly to the traditional form and content of the icon (both of which are canonical) so as to be faithful to what the church believes, teaches, prays, and lives.

At the Second Council of Nicea in 787 AD the entire church, East and West, came together to proclaim that icon is essential to the church's proclamation of the Word, declaring that icon is the very Word of God in line and color. Just as we encounter God in the written text of the sacred scriptures, we meet the Lord and the saints in the painted text of the icon. Every true icon is a *theophany*, a place of graced encounter with the living God, and through the icon, the canonical liturgical art of the undivided church for its first 1000 years, God is worshiped and adored and the holy ones of God, the saints, are venerated.

Thus, every icon is an image which makes the Incarnate Lord visible, either in his own sacred person; in the events of salvation history or in all of those persons, such as Mary, the saints (and ourselves) who have been redeemed, transformed and transfigured by the saving death and resurrection of Jesus. This is the meaning of the veneration of the various icons of Christ liturgically: the altar, the Gospel book; the eucharistic elements, the bishop or priest and the assembly. The painted images of Christ, Mary, or the saints that we call icons make visible for our sake these persons who are always and everywhere invisibly present. Icons present us with a spiritual portrait of those portrayed in them and the stylization of the features and proportions of the figures are deliberate, representing the persons and events of salvation history, who are both of this world and yet already participating the life of the world to come. This transformation, transfiguration, and illumination of every person and the entirety of creation in Christ is symbolized in the icon by light. This is the reason that all of the elements of the icon are luminous with gold or painted highlights that make the human beings, garments, landscape, architectural elements, and background radiant with an interior light.

In the past 30 years the traditional icon has been rediscovered, both by Orthodox and

Eastern Catholic Christians who have never ceased to reverence the icon, and by Roman Catholics and other Western Christians who are discovering in the icon its theological and spiritual depth and beauty. Speaking a silent language beyond the barriers of the words and antagonisms that divide humanity, the icon has emerged as a place of renewed encounter with God, shared prayer and dialogue among Christians and the proclamation of the Gospel, in line and color, to all those seeking the Author of truth, goodness and beauty.

—Charles Rohrbacher
Iconographer

A Contemplative Rosary

A Way of Contemplating the Paschal Mystery

A Contemplative Rosary is intended for both communal and personal prayer. The Our Father, Hail Mary and Glory to the Father are sung to simple chant melodies and the decades/mysteries have accompanying scripture readings and icons. This people's edition adds a further element. Dr. Elaine Park's biblical meditations, designed especially for individual prayer, invite the reader to delve more deeply into each mystery before turning the page to view the icon and pray the decade.

The purpose of all these elements—music, scripture readings, icons and meditations—is to aid contemplation, or to borrow a phrase from John Paul II, "to open up a scenario on which to focus our attention."[1] But what is contemplation? Contemplation is a kind of seeing or "looking at" which heightens our identification and communion with the reality seen. Such seeing happens on many levels. One sees with the eyes, but also with the heart, mind and spirit. One *sees* when one truly *hears* and receives what is spoken. And finally, *acting* on what we have come to see/know, we come to see/know it more profoundly.

As Bishop Warfel stresses in his introduction, contemplation (or mysticism) in this sense is not a specialty for mystics, but a requirement of ordinary Christian living and praying. It describes our relationship to the Word (ultimately, Christ himself) in prayer. When at Eucharist we hear of Christ's encounter with the Samaritan Woman, or the Man Born Blind, or poor Lazarus in the tomb, we do not "look at" these things as though we are looking at a physics problem. Rather, standing with each of these characters, we are "looking at" the face of Christ who looks back. Our own time and story merges with the time and story of the Gospel, for the Risen One addresses us now in these scriptures and seeks our hearts. The object or scenario of contemplation, then, is Christ, or more exactly, the Paschal Mystery of Christ. But we contemplate this one mystery of God's love through the many scenarios of Christ's life. This is what happens in the Eucharist's Liturgy of the Word. This is what happens in praying the psalms, canticles, and readings of the Hours. For we see the psalmist's many situations, yearnings, cries of anguish and joy as foreshadowing and fulfilled in Christ: "Behold, I come to do your will, O God" (Hebrews 10:7; Psalm 40:8–9). The same is true of the rosary's mysteries. In contemplating them, we re-play the details of the Paschal Mystery—

joyful, luminous, sorrowful, and glorious. That is why Paul VI called the rosary a compendium of the Gospel[2] and John Paul II describes it as "contemplating Christ with Mary."[3] Over the beads, we *rehearse* or prayerfully *re-hear (lectio divina!)* the paschal story. Why? Because in baptism we have been called to co-enact this story with Christ: "where I am, there also will my servant be" (John 12:26). The story continues in us. And so as the rosary closes, we pray "that by meditating on these mysteries we may imitate what they contain and obtain what they promise."

Structure and Elements: Postures, Icons, Music, and Scripture

How one prays this rosary may range from large-scale enactment in a church with an assembly, presider, choir, and readers (which takes about 50 minutes) to individual recitation at home. Communal enactment of the rosary could take place several times a year, keyed to the seasons, for example, the joyful mysteries during Advent, the luminous in Ordinary Time, the sorrowful in Lent, and the glorious during Easter Season. Praying together as *church* in this way nourishes and is nourished by personal prayer. So a brief word is offered here about this rosary's structure and elements, emphasizing the communal form of enactment, but also touching upon the alternatives of small-group and individual recitation.

Postures

Since *A Contemplative Rosary* is an extended and reflective prayer, its postures are borrowed from another contemplative prayer form, the Liturgy of the Hours. The primary posture is sitting (for the Hail Marys interspersed with scripture passages). There are also moments for standing and bowing (see chart below). For individual recitation, one may prefer less formal postures, keeping in mind that we pray not only with our heads, but with our bodies.

Icons

Charles Rohrbacher's icon has a large central panel showing the Annunciation, bordered by smaller panels, one for each mystery. It is available in two formats—on an enhanced CD for projection in large spaces and throughout the pages of the people's book. For the rosary's opening and closing, the central panel of the Annunciation may be the visual focus. As each mystery is announced, its specific icon is projected (or viewed in the book) and remains on view during the decade. The people's chants are easily memorized so that our eyes, soon freed from the printed page, can attend to the icon.

Music

The music of this rosary is available in three formats—in the people's book, on a CD, and in a songbook, which includes the complete score for musicians and scripture passages for readers.

Gathering/Preparation: Several pieces may gather and prepare participants for praying the rosary: Craig Kingsbury's evocative instrumental version of the *"Salve Regina,"* the rich, wonderful imagery of Justin Mulcahay's "Mary the Dawn" (a cappella chant), and Pia Moriarty's "Pilgrim Prayer," which reminds us, as Congar once said, that the Christian life is essentially one of pilgrimage, a journey we make not alone but in company with each other, the saints, Mary and Christ.

The Rosary: There are two options for beginning: Form A—an Opening Dialogue based on Psalm 70 (chanted or spoken), and Form B—the Sign of the Cross and Apostles' Creed (spoken). The chants for the Lord's Prayer, Hail Mary, and Glory to the Father are simple and easy to memorize. Consider chanting these prayers even when praying the rosary alone. That is why they appear on the end-page of the meditation book, which also serves as a bookmark while one moves through the mysteries. However, for communal enactment, arrangements have been provided for choir, keyboard, cello, and handbells. As each decade unfolds, the Hail Mary expands from unison to SAT to SATB with handbells. The *"Salve Regina"* and chant settings for the Closing Dialogue and Prayer conclude the rosary. Individuals or small groups may do all these prayers more simply, without harmonies and instrumentation—or pray along with the recorded version.

Sending Forth: After the conclusion of the rosary, "Let It Be Done to Us" may be used for dismissal. This song focuses on Mary as model of the church and of discipleship. In the words of her *fiat,* we pray that we may fulfill our call.

Scripture

The announcement of each mystery is followed by a very brief passage of scripture, which summarizes in advance the overall drift of the mystery, in the same way that the alleluia verse at liturgy puts the whole Gospel in a nutshell. The Our Father is then sung or spoken in response, setting the stage for a more detailed exploration of the mystery. At four points across the decade, scripture passages are presented, unfolding various stages or dimensions of the mystery. Of these four scriptural passages, the first is always musical: sometimes sung by the choir alone, sometimes in combination with the reader. In small-group or individual recitation these passages may be read or spoken. During the Hail Marys following each passage, we contemplate the scripture we have just heard. The resulting pattern or rhythm is one of *repetition* and *variation.* Another way of putting this: the mantra-like repetition of prayers, especially the *Hail Mary,* is a way of sitting still. The variation of the mysteries, elaborated in music, scripture passages, icons and meditations, is a way of taking a journey. So we come into stillness and in this stillness we go on a journey. It is the stillness of Mary before God's Word. It is the journey of the Paschal Mystery, which Mary freely undertook in response to God's Word: "...I am the handmaid of the Lord. May it be done to me according to your word" (Luke 1:38). A chart of *A Contemplative Rosary,* with all the elements described above, is provided on the following page.

—Bob Hurd
San Jose, California
September 2004

---

[1] John Paul II, Apostolic Letter *Rosarium Virginis Mariae* (October 16, 2002), 29.

[2] cf. Paul VI, Apostolic Exhortation *Marialis Cultus* (February 2, 1974).

[3] *Rosarium Virginis Mariae*, chapter 1.

OPENING

Standing

Icon of Annunciation projected

Opening: Form A (Psalm 70) or Form B (Sign of the Cross and Apostles' Creed)

Our Father/3 Hail Marys/Glory to the Father

THE DECADES

Standing

Icon of Mystery projected

Announcement of Mystery and Summary Scripture (Reader)/Our Father

Sitting

1st Scripture Passage (Choir or Choir with Reader)

3 Hail Marys

2nd Scripture Passage (Reader)

3 Hail Marys

3rd Scripture Passage (Reader)

3 Hail Marys

4th Scripture Passage (Reader)

1 Hail Mary

Standing and bowing during "Glory to the Father...Holy Spirit"

Glory to the Father

CLOSING

Standing

Icon of the Annunciation projected

Salve Regina

Closing Dialogue and Prayer

Sign of the Cross and Amen

MARY THE DAWN

Chant

continued on next page

Ma - ry the Bea - con, Christ the Ha - ven's Rest;

Ma - ry the Mir - ror, Christ the Vi - sion Blest!

Ma - ry the Moth - er, Christ the Moth - er's Son.

Both ev - er blest while end - less a - ges run. A - men.

Text by Justin Mulcahy, CP, 1894–1981, under the pseudonym "Paul Cross." Administered by Warner Chappell. All rights reserved. Used with permission. Music: Adaptation of Gregorian Mode IV.

PILGRIM PRAYER

Pia Moriarty

Refrain

Hail Ma - ry, full of grace, bless the jour - ney, bless the place we go to and we leave.

Verses

1. We give praise for the won - der of our God,
2. We give praise for the wis - dom of our God,
3. We give praise for the mer - cy of our God,
4. We give praise for the kind - ness of our God,
5. We give praise for the pa - tience of our God,
6. We give praise for the good - ness of our God,

to Refrain

1. who sends us com - pan - ions on our way.
2. who gives us the free - dom to be - lieve.
3. who lives in the doubt and in the dream.
4. who teach - es us gent - ly to for - give.
5. who heals us in ways we can - not know.
6. who smiles on the pil - grim com - ing home.

The Rosary

making the sign of the cross

OPENING DIALOGUE

Bob Hurd

Our Father
Hail Mary (3)
Glory to the Father

Form B:

Priest/Leader: In the name of the Father, and of the Son, and of the Holy Spirit.
All: Amen.

All: (Apostles' Creed)

I believe in God, the Father almighty,
  creator of heaven and earth.
I believe in Jesus Christ,
  his only Son, our Lord.
He was conceived by the power
  of the Holy Spirit
  and born of the Virgin Mary.
He suffered under Pontius Pilate,
  was crucified, died, and was buried.
He descended to the dead.
On the third day he rose again.

He ascended into heaven,
  and is seated at the
  right hand of the Father.
He will come again
  to judge the living
  and the dead.
I believe in the Holy Spirit,
  the holy catholic Church,
  the communion of saints,
  the forgiveness of sins,
  the resurrection of the body,
  and the life everlasting. Amen.

Our Father
Hail Mary (3)
Glory to the Father

The First Joyful Mystery:

THE ANNUNCIATION
Luke 1:26–38

The first five decades, the "joyful mysteries," are marked by *the joy radiating from the event of the Incarnation.* This is clear from the first mystery, the Annunciation, where Gabriel's greeting to the Virgin of Nazareth is linked to an invitation to messianic joy: "Rejoice, Mary." The whole of salvation history, in some sense the entire history of the world, has led up to this greeting.

Pope John Paul II,
The Rosary of the Virgin Mary
(*Rosarium Virginis Mariae*), 20

---

*T*he mystery of the incarnation opens with the message of the angel Gabriel to a young virgin in the Galilean city of Nazareth. Although Luke calls Nazareth a "city," it was really just a small village with a single well, and whose inhabitants grew their own food, sewed their own clothing, shared facilities such as threshing floor and olive press, and paid taxes from their limited resources. The young virgin of Nazareth would have participated in all the domestic tasks of village life, many of them requiring stamina as she worked side-by-side with the townsfolk of Nazareth.

The virgin's name is Mary, or Miriam, a popular Jewish name recalling her Biblical ancestor. As a young Jewish woman, Mary undoubtedly learned the ancient Psalm prayers and knew the stories of the God who had acted throughout the history of the Jewish people. She would have celebrated the sabbath each week as well as other traditional feasts at home, in the synagogue and in the Jerusalem temple. With the other people of the village, Mary would have found great comfort in the covenant relationship with God which bound the people both with God and with one another.

The angel Gabriel first greets the virgin of Nazareth, not by her Jewish name, but by another designation, "woman ever-favored," *kecharitomene*, in the Greek of the New Testament. *Kecharitomene* means one who has been exceedingly favored, or graced abundantly, indicating that the favor is freely given, and that its effects are long-standing. The angel says further why Mary is called *kecharitomene*: she is favored because "the Lord is with you." The angelic announcement thus is not only of something new that God is about to do, but it is also a declaration about what has been true all along: God's presence in the life of Mary. She is a woman favored by God, having already lived as recipient of God's favor and God's abiding presence. Through the angel, the God who is always present promises that Mary, though a virgin, will conceive and bear a son, and that her cousin Elizabeth, though barren, is already in her sixth month.

In response to the angel's message Mary says, "...I am the handmaid of the Lord. May it be done to me according to your word" (Luke 1:38). In her response of fervent obedience, Mary refers to herself as a "servant," or, more precisely, a "slave." With this self-designation, Mary indicates not only her humble stance before God, but most likely her own lived experience in Nazareth as well. As a servant of God, Mary is one who puts herself totally in God's service, promising and living in obedience even when she doesn't understand. Her response is a "yes" to all that God has done, is doing, and will do. Mary's self-identification as maidservant does not imply that she is passive or lacking in initiative, but is a young woman who responds freely and confidently and with a readiness to serve. Throughout her life, Mary's being a servant of the Lord entailed a service characterized by joy and fidelity, embracing attentiveness to God and attentiveness to God's people.

Miriam of Nazareth, God's favored one and God's servant, is chosen to be the mother of one called Jesus, Son of the Most High, and Son of God. Her ready acceptance of the angelic message shows all of us how to be servants of God and sets in motion the great story of God's entry into our world in human flesh, the story of our salvation.

FOR REFLECTION

Like Mary, each of us is graced in many ways. How has God graced your life? How do you respond to God's gracious activity?

When Mary identifies herself as the servant of the Lord, she says "yes" to whatever God asks of her. How do you show in your own life that you are ready to do what God asks?

The First Joyful Mystery: The Annunciation

The First Joyful Mystery:
The Annunciation

(STAND)

The Lord himself will give you this sign:
the virgin shall conceive, and bear a son,
and shall name him Immanuel.

(Isaiah 7:14)

Our Father

(SIT)

The angel Gabriel was sent from God to a town of Galilee called Nazareth
to a virgin betrothed to a man named Joseph of the house of David,
and the virgin's name was Mary. And coming to her, he said,
"Hail favored one! The Lord is with you."
But she was greatly troubled at what was said
and pondered what sort of greeting this might be.

(Luke 1:26–29)

Hail Mary (3)

Then the angel said to her, "Do not be afraid, Mary,
for you have found favor with God.
Behold, you will conceive in your womb and bear a son,
and you shall name him Jesus."

(Luke 1:30–31)

Hail Mary (3)

But Mary said to the angel. "How can this be, since I have no relations with a man?"
And the angel said to her in reply, "The holy Spirit will come upon you,
and the power of the Most High will overshadow you.
Therefore the child to be born will be called holy, the Son of God."

(Luke 1:35)

Hail Mary (3)

Mary said,
"Behold, I am the handmaid of the Lord.
May it be done to me according to your word."

(Luke 1:38)

Hail Mary (1)

(STAND)

Glory to the Father

The Second Joyful Mystery:

THE VISITATION
Luke 1:39–56

Moved by charity, Mary goes to the house of her kinswoman. When Mary enters, Elizabeth replies to her greeting and feels the child leap in her womb, and being "filled with the Holy Spirit" she greets Mary with a loud cry: "Blessed are you among women, and blessed is the fruit of your womb!" (cf. Luke 1:40–42). Elizabeth's exclamation or acclamation was subsequently to become part of the Hail Mary, as a continuation of the angel's greeting, thus becoming one of the Church's most frequently used prayers.

Pope John Paul II,
Mother of the Redeemer
(Redemptoris Mater), 12

---

*I*n the Second Joyful Mystery, the Visitation, Mary hastens to her cousin Elizabeth in the hill country of Judah. Both the Gospel of Luke and the Acts of Apostles are structured around journeys, with one great journey from Galilee to Jerusalem in the Gospel, and from Jerusalem to Rome in Acts. Mary is the first person in the Gospel to set out on a journey, one which she undertook with eager decisiveness, difficult as the travel would be.

In the Judean hill country, Elizabeth and her unborn child are recipients of the good news brought by the angel Gabriel to Mary, and now brought by Mary to her elderly cousin. Mary thus becomes the first person to carry both the words of good news and the very presence of the good news within her. Elizabeth, filled with the Holy Spirit, joyfully recognizes this Gospel when she proclaims that Mary is "mother of my Lord," simultaneously honoring both mother and child.

To the initial descriptions of Mary as woman ever-favored, servant of God, and mother of the Lord, Elizabeth adds another description: Mary is a believer. "Believer" is a fundamental way of describing disciples throughout the New Testament and one of the names for the church (e.g., Acts of the Apostles 2:44) More than an adherence to a creed or set of dogmas, belief embraces a totality of response, a commitment of one's whole person to the one in whom belief is placed. It is a relational response, characterized by fidelity. As a woman of faith, Mary is placed centrally among all those who believe; she presents a model for believers and becomes an image of the church.

In the visitation account, Mary expresses her belief first by her bringing the good news to Elizabeth, and then by her Spirit-filled prayer in which she announces that her very being is magnifying the Lord. One of the best loved prayers in the Christian tradition, the *Magnificat* is both song and poetry in which Mary draws on words, images, and style from ancient Jewish prayers, adding new words that flow from contemplation of her own experience. When something is magnified, what is already there becomes more evident; it is enlarged for those who would not otherwise see all the details. That is precisely what Mary does in the *Magnificat*. She magnifies, heightens, amplifies the image of God in such a way that those of us who are nearsighted or myopic can see more clearly who God is and how God acts.

The God whom Mary magnifies is clearly the same God who came to be known throughout the Hebrew Scriptures. Mary specifically identifies God as the God of Israel and she recalls persons and events of Jewish history. The God of Israel is faithful to ancient promises, and imparts mercy generation after generation. In the *Magnificat*, Mary proclaims joyfully that the God who had acted powerfully in the past to save the oppressed people is continuing to act in a new and powerful way. Most specifically, God repeatedly acts for the benefit of those who are lowly, impoverished, and hungry. What Mary expresses in the psalm is not only a recital of her own experience of God, but she also presents a picture of the way that God has acted in the past, is acting in the present, and will continue to act in the future. Mary's prayer is another message of good news.

FOR REFLECTION

At the visitation, Mary expresses her faith both by decisive action and by profound prayerfulness. How do you, as an individual and as a part of a believing community, combine action and prayer in your own faith life? How could you express your faith more clearly and vibrantly?

Mary announces the message of God's constant care for the poor, a message that Jesus proclaims in the synagogue at Nazareth. Read and reflect on Jesus' good news to the poor (Luke 4:16–21). Where do you see yourself?

The Second Joyful Mystery: The Visitation

The Second Joyful Mystery:
The Visitation

(STAND)

...the moment the sound of your greeting reached my ears,
the infant in my womb leapt for joy.

(Luke 1:44)

Our Father

(SIT)

(chanted to the melody of Puer Nobis)
In haste to Judah Mary went
to see her cousin Elizabeth,
who in old age conceived a son,
a prophet of the Most High One.

When Mary's greeting reached her kin,
with joy the baby leapt within.
Thus did the grace of God abound
so let our songs of praise resound.

(based on Luke 1:36, 39–41a)

Hail Mary (3)

...and Elizabeth, filled with the holy Spirit,
cried out in a loud voice and said,
"Blessed are you among women,
and blessed is the fruit of your womb."

(Luke 1:41b–42)

Hail Mary (3)

Blessed are you who believed
that what was spoken to you by the Lord would be fulfilled.

(Luke 1:45)

Hail Mary (3)

And Mary said:
"My soul proclaims the greatness of the Lord;
my spirit rejoices in God my savior."

(Luke 1:46)

Hail Mary (1)

(STAND)

Glory to the Father

The Third Joyful Mystery:

THE NATIVITY OF JESUS
Luke 2:1–20

As guardian of the mystery "hidden for ages in the mind of God," which begins to unfold before his eyes "in the fullness of time," Joseph, together with Mary, is a privileged witness to the birth of the Son of God into the world… Joseph was an eyewitness to this birth, which took place in conditions that, humanly speaking, were embarrassing—a first announcement of that "self-emptying" (cf. Philippians 2:5–8) which Christ freely accepted for the forgiveness of sins.

Pope John Paul II,
*Guardian of the Redeemer
(Redemptoris Custos)*, 10

---

*T*he first two joyful mysteries prepare the way for the central mystery, the coming of the Savior into our world. Heaven and earth, majesty and lowliness, divinity and humanity, joy and wonder are all brought together in this event. Having already made a journey to her cousin Elizabeth in the Judean hill country, Mary again travels, this time from Nazareth to Bethlehem. In this city of David, she gives birth to the promised child in the humblest of circumstances, with a manger for his bed, and simple swaddling for his clothing. News of the child's lowly birth is first brought to shepherds who, like the child, have a lowly place in society. Already at Jesus' birth, his mother's prophetic declaration that God exalts those of low degree is being fulfilled. The angelic announcement to the shepherds clearly stresses that the child has import far beyond what his humble birth would suggest. The child is good news for "all the people." He is born "for you." His birth is at once glory in heaven and peace on earth.

At the heart of the angelic message is a proclamation of Jesus' identity as Savior, Christ, and Lord. The angel Gabriel, in the annunciation to Mary at Nazareth, had already identified the promised child by his name Jesus, as Son of the Most High, and as Son of God. Now the joyful declaration to the shepherds reveals that the *promise-announced* to Mary has become the *promise-fulfilled* at Jesus' birth. The child lying in the manger is Savior, as his name "Jesus" indicates. He is the hoped-for Davidic descendant called the Christ. And he has such a close relationship with God that he even shares with God the title "Lord," foreshadowing the full revelation of Jesus' Lordship that will be seen in his resurrection and exaltation.

The shepherds' immediate response to the heavenly message is to journey in haste to see what had been made known to them. Their haste is reminiscent of Mary's earlier setting out in haste to go to her cousin Elizabeth. For shepherds and Mary alike, such promptness suggests an eager welcome of the message, as well as urgency to proclaim with wonder and joy the good news they have received.

For Mary, wonder and joy are joined with contemplation, as she ponders in her heart. In the language of the New Testament, the word for *ponder* suggests a very active reflecting, much like holding a prism in sunlight and delighting in the variety of light and color that can be observed, turning the prism to encounter new lights from every angle. At the birth of her son, Mary ponders the words and events she has experienced, penetrating the mystery of her son ever more deeply. For Mary, the enlightening that arises from meditation draws her more profoundly into the mystery and extends beyond herself. She becomes a source of enlightenment for others as she makes known her son and God's saving presence in him.

FOR REFLECTION

Who is this child? What significance do the various names, titles and descriptions of the newborn child have for you? Do you have a favored way of addressing Jesus in prayer? What does the name signify for you?

Mary treasured all the words and events about Jesus, pondering them in her heart. How and when do you reflect on the mysteries of the faith? How do you share the light from your own contemplation?

The Third Joyful Mystery: The Nativity

The Third Joyful Mystery:
The Nativity

(STAND)

And the Word became flesh and made his dwelling among us…

(John 1:14)

Our Father

(SIT)

(chanted to the melody of Puer Natus)
To Bethlehem went Joseph, alleluia,
with Mary, his betrothed, alleluia, alleluia.
And there her time was come; she gave birth to her firstborn son,
and laid him in the manger.

To shepherds watching o'er their sheep, alleluia,
the angel of the Lord did speak, alleluia, alleluia.
Behold, I bring good news, the ancient promise now come true:
today is born the savior.

(based on Luke 2:1–11)

Hail Mary (3)

And suddenly there was a multitude of heavenly hosts with the angel,
praising God and saying:
"Glory to God in the highest
and on earth peace to those on whom his favor rests."

(Luke 2:13–14)

Hail Mary (3)

So they went in haste and found Mary and Joseph,
and the infant lying in the manger.
When they saw this, they made known the message
that had been told them about this child.

(Luke 2:16–17)

Hail Mary (3)

And Mary kept all these things, reflecting on them in her heart.

(Luke 2:19)

Hail Mary (1)

(STAND)

Glory to the Father

The Fourth Joyful Mystery:

THE PRESENTATION
Luke 2:21–40

In the episode of the Presentation of Jesus in the Temple (cf. Luke 2:22–35), the Church, guided by the Spirit, has detected, over and above the fulfillment of the laws regarding the offering of the firstborn (cf. Exodus 13:11–16) and the purification of the mother (cf. Leviticus 12:6–8), a mystery of salvation related to the history of salvation…The church has seen the universal nature of salvation proclaimed, for Simeon, greeting in the Child the light to enlighten the peoples and the glory of the people Israel (cf. Luke 2:32), recognized in the Messiah, the Savior of all.

Pope Paul VI,
For the Right Ordering and Development
of Devotion to the Blessed Virgin Mary
(Marialis Cultus), 20

---

*W*hen Mary and Joseph present Jesus in the temple in Jerusalem, Luke depicts them, along with Simeon and Anna, as devout, hopeful Jewish women and men. As typical Jewish parents, Mary and Joseph act in accordance with the law of Moses by bringing their child to the temple and offering sacrifice to the Lord. Coming from the small village of Nazareth, its inhabitants numbered among the poor of the land, Mary and Joseph bring the offering assigned to their social class: two turtledoves or young pigeons. In spite of their seeming lack of importance, parents and child are recognized by the righteous and devout Simeon. Describing himself as "servant of God," as Mary had at the annunciation, Simeon is in God's attendance as he awaits the consolation of Israel. The final character in the scene, the prophetess Anna, is noted for her fidelity in serving the Lord in the temple night and day, and for fasting and prayer. Through these descriptions, Luke situates the story of Jesus within the story of God's faithful covenanted people who are now responding with piety and hope to a new manifestation of God's saving activity in Jesus.

In this Fourth Joyful Mystery, the Presentation, there is no angelic messenger to proclaim the child's identity as at the annunciation and birth of Jesus. Rather, the revealer and one directing the action in the temple is the Holy Spirit who rests upon Simeon, makes known to him that he will not see death until he has seen the Christ, and prompts him to go into the temple. That same Spirit is the source of inspiration for Simeon's canticle in which he adds to the depiction of Jesus by identifying him as revelation to the Gentiles and glory for Israel. The elderly prophetess Anna is assuredly Spirit-filled as well, for the Spirit is the origin of prophetic speech throughout the biblical story. In her own Spirit-inspired speech, Anna speaks about Jesus to all awaiting the redemption of Jerusalem. These Spirit-filled human characters, just as much as angelic messengers, are the means by which God makes the promised child known in the world.

Even in the context of the great joy and consolation of God's people, this scene offers a glimpse of the shadow of sorrow to come. While the child is destined to be both revelation and glory, he will also be associated with the falling and rising of many. The infant so readily welcomed by the shepherds and by Simeon and Anna will be spoken against and resisted. Simeon's brief prophecy foretells future opposition to Jesus that will divide the people. Moreover, that a sword will pierce the very being of his mother. Whatever this prophesied sword may denote, Mary would surely have continued to ponder the meaning of Simeon's prophecy and what it would mean for her son and for her people. As if to offer reassurance that opposition to Jesus is not the final word, Luke ends the account of the presentation with the prophetess Anna giving thanks at sight of the child and proclaiming him to all those hoping for redemption.

FOR REFLECTION

The Holy Spirit is active in the scene of Jesus' presentation—directing, prompting, and inspiring. How do you see the action and presence of the Spirit of God in your own experience?

Simeon and Anna, like the angelic messengers in earlier scenes, are the source of proclaiming Jesus' identity and significance. How do you share in the task of proclaiming Jesus?

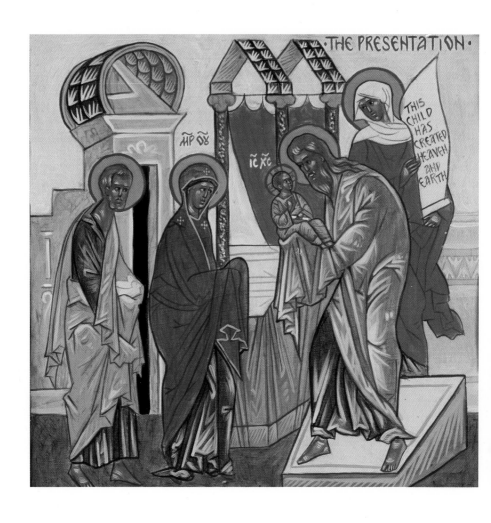

The Fourth Joyful Mystery: The Presentation

The Fourth Joyful Mystery:
The Presentation

(STAND)

When [Christ] came into the world, he said:…
"Behold, O come to do your will, O God."

(Hebrews 10:5, 7b)

Our Father

(SIT)

They took [Jesus] up to Jerusalem to present him to the Lord.
Now there was a man in Jerusalem whose name was Simeon….It had
been revealed to him by the holy Spirit that he should not see death
before he had seen the Messiah of the Lord.

(Luke 2:22, 25–26)

Hail Mary (3)

[Simeon] took the child in his arms and blessed God, saying:
"Now Master, you may let your servant go
in peace, according to your word,
for my eyes have seen your salvation…".

(Luke 2:28–30a)

Hail Mary (3)

And Simeon…said to Mary his mother,
"Behold, this child is destined for the fall and rise of many in Israel
and to be a sign that will be contradicted
(and you yourself a sword will pierce)
so that the thoughts of many hearts may be revealed."

(Luke 2:34–35)

Hail Mary (3)

…they returned to Galilee, to their own town of Nazareth.
The child grew and became strong, filled with wisdom;
and the favor of God was upon him.

(Luke 2:39b–40)

Hail Mary (1)

(STAND)

Glory to the Father

The Fifth Joyful Mystery:
THE FINDING OF JESUS IN THE TEMPLE
Luke 2:41–52

Joy mixed with drama marks the fifth mystery, the finding of the twelve-year-old Jesus in the Temple. Here He appears in His divine wisdom as he listens and raises questions, already in effect one who "teaches." The revelation of His mystery as the Son wholly dedicated to his Father's affairs proclaims the radical nature of the Gospel, in which even the closest of human relationships are challenged by the absolute demands of the Kingdom. Mary and Joseph, fearful and anxious, "did not understand" His words (Luke 2:50).

Pope John Paul II,
*The Rosary of the Virgin Mary
(Rosarium Virginis Mariae), 20*

---

*T*he years following Jesus' birth and infancy pass with little note in Luke's Gospel. Luke says simply that the child grew and was filled with wisdom and the grace of God. The Fifth Joyful Mystery, the Finding in the Temple, illustrates both the wisdom and grace of God active within the young Jesus.

Continuing to show fidelity to their traditions as they had in presenting Jesus in the temple, each year his parents went to Jerusalem for celebration of the Passover. Jesus follows Jewish custom as well, journeying with them when he is twelve years of age. The family would have traveled with other Jewish pilgrims, praying the pilgrimage psalms according to custom, rejoicing at the sight of the holy city. The gospel journeys for Mary, Joseph and Jesus, as well as for Jesus' followers, express commitment to religious traditions, a readiness to be of service, and a desire to proclaim the good news to all people.

As a young woman in Nazareth, Mary had faced all the difficulties associated with economic insecurity and political domination, sharing the experience of so many of the world's poor. In this situation, Mary again shares a common human reality. Like many mothers and fathers, she feels the agony of a lost child and understands neither his actions nor his words. When Jesus is not found among the pilgrims returning from Jerusalem, Mary and Joseph search for him anxiously and question his actions. Jesus' response to Mary's concerned questioning is enigmatic to his parents as well as to all those who have tried to understand his reply. When Mary does not comprehend, Jesus' words become a source for contemplation, just as the earlier events of his birth had been the wellspring for her reflection. Mary's habit of meditating on the mysteries must have begun in Nazareth, where the weekly celebration of the Sabbath created a rhythm of regular immersion into the deepest realities of God's abiding presence and care.

As Mary pondered Jesus' words she would have seen several possibilities of meaning. His words could indicate that he is in his Father's house, that he is about his Father's affairs or business, or even that he is among those who belong to his Father. At the Annunciation, Mary had learned of Jesus' identity as Son of God, and now his reply to her question reveals something about that sonship. His words, an expression of Jesus' wisdom and grace, affirm his unique place in his Father's saving plan, his active role therein, and his distinctly personal bond with God. Jesus' reply to Mary are his first words in Luke's Gospel and highlight the relationship that will be developed throughout the whole story of his life, death, and resurrection. Following on this statement, Luke shows that Jesus is ever in communion with God, frequently at prayer and speaking directly to his Father, even at the final moments of his life. No matter what the circumstances, Jesus dwells in his Father's house and must be involved in his Father's concerns.

FOR REFLECTION

When Mary doesn't understand Jesus' words, she meditates on them. How do you respond to mysteries that you don't understand?

Jesus and his Father are always concerned with the needs of all. Reflect on how God's abiding concern is manifest in your life, in the life of the church, and in the world. Pray in praise, thanksgiving and petition.

The Fifth Joyful Mystery: The Finding of Jesus in the Temple

The Fifth Joyful Mystery:
The Finding of Jesus in the Temple

(STAND)

The Lord GOD has given me
a well-trained tongue,
That I might know how to speak to the weary
a word that will rouse them.
(Isaiah 50:4ab)

Our Father

(SIT)

Each year Jesus' parents went up to Jerusalem for the feast of Passover,
and when he was twelve years old, they went up according to festival custom.
After they had completed its days, as they were returning,
the boy Jesus remained behind in Jerusalem, but his parents did not know it.
Thinking that he was in the caravan, they journeyed for a day and looked for him
among their relatives and acquaintances…
(Luke 2:41–44)

Hail Mary (3)

…but not finding him, they returned to Jerusalem to look for him.
After three days they found him in the temple,
sitting in the midst of the teachers, listening to them and asking them questions,
and all who heard him were astounded at his understanding and his answers.
(Luke 2:45–46)

Hail Mary (3)

…and his mother said to him, "Son, why have you done this to us?
Your father and I have been looking for you with great anxiety."
And he said to them, "Why were you looking for me?
Did you not know I must be in my Father's house?"
(Luke 2:48b–49)

Hail Mary (3)

He went down with them and came to Nazareth, and was obedient to them;
and his mother kept all these things in her heart.
And Jesus advanced [in] wisdom and age and favor before God and man.
(Luke 2:51–52)

Hail Mary (1)

(STAND)

Glory to the Father

The First Luminous Mystery:

THE BAPTISM OF JESUS
Matthew 3:13–17; Mark 1:9–11; Luke 3:21–22; John 1:29–34

The Baptism in the Jordan is first of all a mystery of light. Here, as Christ descends into the waters, the innocent one who became "sin" for our sake (cf. II Corinthians 5:21), the heavens open wide and the voice of the Father declares him the beloved Son (cf. Matthew 3:17 and parallels), while the Spirit descends on him to invest him with the mission which he is to carry out.

Pope John Paul II,
The Rosary of the Virgin Mary
(Rosarium Virginis Mariae), 21

---

*T*he First Luminous Mystery, the Baptism of Jesus in the Jordan, reveals with strong imagery that Jesus is God's own son, beloved and well-pleasing. The event also displays Jesus' oneness with us, sinless though he was.

Before Jesus began his public ministry, John the Baptist was preaching in the Judean wilderness, calling the people to repentance and baptizing them in the Jordan River. Though the hopeful crowds were following John, thinking that he might be the Christ, John himself recognized that his role was to prepare the way. John was not the Light, but he was to bear witness to the Light (John 1:8). Even as he baptized with water, John announced that one who is greater would baptize with the Holy Spirit and with fire. With humble clarity, John declares that the one who is coming is superior to him, and his baptism is more powerful.

John preached a baptism of repentance, and those whom he baptized confessed their sins. John's baptism would bring them forgiveness. Thus when Jesus appears before John to be baptized, John objects that he, not Jesus, is the one who should be baptized. Yet Jesus insists. Although he is greater than John, Jesus freely chooses to be baptized, associating himself with weak and sinful humanity. He needs baptism neither as a sign of repentance nor for forgiveness of sins, but by his baptism, Jesus unites himself with all of us.

Jesus' baptism reveals even more vividly his unique relationship with his Father. The ripping apart of the heavens dramatically displays an end to the separation between God and humanity, for in Jesus there is a new presence of God's power among us. The descending of the Spirit in the form of a dove and the voice from heaven unveil for us the reality of Jesus' identity: he is son of God on whom God's own Spirit rests. The Spirit who descends on Jesus at his baptism remains always present and active in him, a sign of God's continuing communion and favor. All that is heard and seen in the event confirms John's declaration about Jesus: he is the one people had awaited for long centuries, and is indeed even greater than their hopes had imagined.

In addition to revealing Jesus' identity as the beloved son of God, his baptism points also to the meaning of baptism for his followers. At baptism each of us, like Jesus, receives the Holy Spirit and becomes a beloved son or daughter of God. The gift of the Spirit given at baptism empowers us to continue Jesus' own saving mission and brings us into union with God and one another. Each of us, through baptism, has "put on Christ," and is one in him (see Galatians 3: 26–28). At our baptism, we are immersed into the mystery of Christ's death and resurrection. Saint Paul wrote to the Roman church about this new reality, saying that we have been buried with Christ, have been baptized into his death, and will also be raised to newness of life and resurrection (see Romans 6: 3–11). Through baptism, we live as members of the body of Christ, with Christ radiating in all that we do. Let us pray that, by the presence and power of the Holy Spirit, we may live our baptismal identity and promises fully, faithfully and joyfully.

FOR REFLECTION

Reflect on Jesus' baptism. How does the event illuminate Jesus' relationship both with God and with us?

Reflect on your own baptism. How do you live in fidelity to your baptismal promises?

The First Luminous Mystery: The Baptism of Jesus

The First Luminous Mystery:
The Baptism of Jesus

(STAND)

No one can enter the kingdom of God without being born of water and Spirit.

(John 3:5)

Our Father

(SIT)

...the people were filled with expectation, and all were asking in their hearts
whether John might be the Messiah; John answered them all saying:
"I am baptizing you with water, but one mightier than I is coming.
I am not worthy to loosen the thongs of his sandals.
He will baptize you with the holy Spirit and fire."

(Luke 3:15–16)

Hail Mary (3)

Then Jesus came from Galilee to John at the Jordan to be baptized by him.
John tried to prevent him, saying,
"I need to be baptized by you, and yet you are coming to me?"

(Matthew 3:13–14)

Hail Mary (3)

After Jesus was baptized, he came up from the water and behold,
the heavens were opened [for him],
and he saw the Spirit of God descending like a dove [and] coming upon him.

(Matthew 3:16)

Hail Mary (3)

And a voice came from the heavens, saying,
"This is my beloved Son, with whom I am well pleased."

(Matthew 3:17)

Hail Mary (1)

(STAND)

Glory to the Father

The Second Luminous Mystery:
THE WEDDING FEAST AT CANA
John 2:1–11

Mary is present at Cana in Galilee as the Mother of Jesus, and in a significant way she contributes to that "beginning of signs" which reveal the messianic power of her Son…the description of the Cana event outlines what is actually manifested as a new kind of motherhood according to the spirit and not just according to the flesh, that is to say Mary's solicitude for human beings, her coming to them in the wide variety of their wants and needs.

Pope John Paul II,
Mother of the Redeemer
(Redemptoris Mater), 21

---

*T*he Second Luminous Mystery, the Wedding at Cana, recalls the first of Jesus' signs, brought about at the request of his mother. Jesus' action shows him continuing the saving signs done by his Father, and reveals something of Jesus identity and mission.

Throughout the Hebrew Scriptures, God effected signs and wonders and deeds of power that transformed the oppression and distress of the chosen people. With a mighty hand, God freed them from slavery, fed them in the desert, and brought them to their own land. Before they entered that land, Moses reminded the people, "…the LORD…wrought before our eyes signs and wonders…" (Deuteronomy 6:22). Although God had multiplied signs through Moses, the people were slow to believe, and even rebelled against Moses and against God.

Just as the God of the Exodus had performed great signs, the son of God responded to human need through signs and wonders and deeds of power. And as the mighty wonders that God worked often resulted in denial and rejection, so, too, did the wonders that Jesus accomplished. Although Jesus did great signs before the people, many still did not believe in him (see John 12:37). At the first of his signs, however, his disciples began to believe.

Jesus' action at Cana, like other signs in the biblical tradition, is not limited to one meaning, but discloses multiple mysteries of faith. The ordinary, discernible realities of water and word that Jesus uses are signs of the extraordinary, hidden realities of God's compassion, overwhelming generosity, and glory. Physical and temporal things become a sign of the spiritual and eternal. When Jesus changes the water into the best of wine, he provides for the people in abundance, a sign of joy and of God's provident care. The choice wine may also remind us of the eucharistic wine which Jesus offers to his followers. Moreover, his presence and intervention at the marriage feast is a sign of God's affirmation of the loving union between husband and wife. Jesus' one sign at Cana thus opens our eyes to many dimensions of God's saving action present in Jesus.

Along with being a multi-faceted sign about Jesus, the wedding feast also shows us an ideal response to him. While some people refused to believe in Jesus even after he had performed many signs, his mother shows absolute confidence in him and believes in the power of his word even before he accomplished any signs. In addition, her faith in Jesus leads her to seek his help for the benefit of others, trusting that he will respond to their need. Her reliance on Jesus is the catalyst that moves him to act. After Jesus transforms the water into wine, his disciples, too, believe in him, showing openness and readiness to follow him. From this perspective, Jesus' sign transforms not only the water, but also transforms the disciples' lack of belief into belief.

We, along with the disciples, get a glimpse of Jesus' glory at Cana and throughout his ministry, and in his Passion and resurrection. Yet his signs and manifestation of glory that began at Cana did not cease with his death and resurrection. He continues to reveal his glory and abiding presence to us through sacramental signs, through his living word, and through the present-day community of disciples who, like the disciples at Cana, are transformed by his power.

FOR REFLECTION

Reflect on the revelation about Jesus at Cana. What are the most important things his first sign reveals to you about Jesus' mission and identity? How do you see Jesus' actions to be like those of God in the Hebrew Scriptures?

Reflect on the revelation about discipleship at Cana. What things assist you in deepening your belief in Jesus?

The Second Luminous Mystery: The Wedding at Cana

The Second Luminous Mystery:
The Wedding at Cana

Let anyone who thirsts, come to me and drink.

(John 7:37)

Our Father

There was a wedding in Cana of Galilee, and the mother of Jesus was there.
…When the wine ran short, [she] said to him, "They have no wine."
[And] Jesus said to her: "Woman, how does your concern affect me?
My hour has not yet come."
His mother said to the servers, "Do whatever he tells you."

(John 2:1, 3–5)

Hail Mary (3)

Jesus told them, "Fill the jars with water."
So they filled them to the brim.
Then he told them, "Draw some out now and take it to the headwaiter."

(John 2:7–8)

Hail Mary (3)

When the headwaiter tasted the water that had become wine,
[he] called the bridegroom and said to him,
"Everyone serves good wine first, and then when people have drunk freely,
an inferior one; but you have kept the good wine until now."

(John 2:9–10)

Hail Mary (3)

Jesus did this as the beginning of his signs at Cana in Galilee
and so revealed his glory,
and his disciples began to believe in him.

(John 2:11)

Hail Mary (1)

Glory to the Father

The Third Luminous Mystery:

THE PROCLAMATION OF THE KINGDOM OF GOD
Mark 1:15; Luke 7:22, 36–50

The sharing in Christ's kingly mission, that is to say the fact of rediscovering in oneself and others the special dignity of our vocation can be described as "kingship". This dignity is expressed in readiness to serve, in keeping with the example of Christ, who "came not to be served but to serve". If, in the light of this attitude of Christ's, "being a king" is truly possible only by "being a servant" then "being a servant" also demands so much spiritual maturity that it must really be described as "being a king".

Pope John Paul II,
Redeemer of Man
(Redemptor Hominis), 21

"*T*his is the time of fulfillment. The kingdom of God is at hand" (Mark 1:15). Throughout his ministry, and even from the cross, Jesus revealed that the coming of God's kingdom is good news that must be welcomed with the eagerness and confidence of a little child. In the Third Luminous Mystery, the Proclamation of the Kingdom of God, we remember how Jesus proclaimed by both word and deed the Gospel of the kingdom of God, and that he calls us to repent and believe this good news.

In the time of Jesus, as well as in the millennia before and after, kingdoms of this world have often been known for brutal domination, for the privilege of a few and the exploitation of the many. Kings and queens of this world have had power to punish and put to death, to capture and enslave, to condemn and to disregard. Even common people have established their own "little kingdoms" in which they exercise power and control, whether it be political, military, religious or psychological. In Jesus' proclamation of God's kingdom, we see a dramatic contrast with the kingdoms of this world. The kingdom of God is a kingdom not *of* this world, even as it is made present *in* this world through the person of Jesus. Jesus tells his disciples that while the great sovereigns of this age use their power over others, his disciples must, like Jesus himself, become servants of one another (Mark 10:42–45). Unlike the rulers of this world, Jesus welcomes the little ones and shows compassion on those who suffer. He reveals his special concern for the outcast by embracing the unclean and by sharing table-fellowship with sinners. In contrast to the sneering shock of the religious elite who consider themselves to be holy, Jesus humbly accepts anointing by a woman known to be a sinner. Instead of condemnation, he announces forgiveness.

Whenever people experience the domination of the kingdoms of this world, they long for deliverance. Ruled by one foreign power after another, the Jews in Jesus' day were looking for the one sent by God to establish a reign of justice and to release them from oppression. When they asked Jesus if he was the one they were awaiting, he answered by describing the signs that God's reign had indeed come: the blind see, the lame walk, lepers are made clean, the deaf hear, those who have died are being raised, and the poor have the good news brought to them (see Luke 7:22). As Jesus establishes God's reign, he releases people from whatever is enslaving and oppressing them, particularly by freeing them from the captivity of sin and selfishness.

The reign of God which has already begun in Jesus will be brought to perfection when he comes again in glory. Inaugurated by Jesus, the kingdom continues to grow mysteriously and certainly as God's saving rule reaches every age and every land. Until Jesus comes again, we, his disciples, are entrusted with the mysteries of the kingdom and are commissioned to continue Jesus' ministry of bringing good news to the poor, of welcoming the outcast, and of offering forgiveness. God gives to us a two-fold grace: the grace of God's saving kingdom among us which we are to receive with conversion of heart and faith; and the grace of extending that rule through our own proclamation of the kingdom of God.

FOR REFLECTION

What do you consider the most important aspects of the kingdom of God as proclaimed by Jesus? How do you manifest those aspects in your own life?

Reflect on the two-fold grace of God's kingdom. How do you welcome the kingdom? How do extend the kingdom?

The Third Luminous Mystery: The Proclamation of the Kingdom of God

The Third Luminous Mystery:
The Proclamation of the Kingdom of God

(STAND)

...know this: the kingdom of God is at hand.

(Luke 10:11)

Our Father

(SIT)

He went around all of Galilee,...proclaiming the gospel of the kingdom,
and curing...disease and illness among the people.

(Matthew 4:23)

Hail Mary (3)

Now there was a sinful woman in the city
who learned he was at table in the house of the Pharisee.
Bringing an alabaster flask of ointment,
she stood behind him at his feet weeping
and began to bathe his feet with her tears.
Then she wiped them with her hair, kissed them,
and anointed them with the ointment.

(Luke 7:37–38)

Hail Mary (3)

When the Pharisee who had invited him saw this he said to himself,
"If this man were a prophet, he would know who and what sort of woman
this is who is touching him, that she is a sinner.

(Luke 7:39)

Hail Mary (3)

[Jesus] said to her, "Your sins are forgiven."
The others at table said to themselves,
"Who is this who even forgives sins?"

(Luke 7:48–49)

Hail Mary (1)

(STAND)

Glory to the Father

The Fourth Luminous Mystery:

THE TRANSFIGURATION
Matthew 17:1–9; Mark 9:2–9; Luke 9:28–36

The mystery of light *par excellence* is the Transfiguration, traditionally believed to have taken place on Mount Tabor. The glory of the Godhead shines forth from the face of Christ as the Father commands the astonished Apostles to "listen to him" (cf. Luke 9:35 and parallels) and to prepare to experience with him the agony of the Passion, so as to come with him to the joy of the Resurrection and a life transfigured by the Holy Spirit.

Pope John Paul II,
The Rosary of the Virgin Mary
(Rosarium Virginis Mariae), 21

---

*E*ach of the Luminous Mysteries, Pope John Paul II tells us, is a revelation of the kingdom now present in the very person of Jesus. In the Fourth Luminous Mystery, the Transfiguration, we hear echoes of the first three mysteries. As at Jesus' baptism, a voice from the heavens identifies Jesus as God's beloved Son. Jesus reveals his glory as he had done at the wedding feast of Cana. And Jesus' transformed appearance, radiant in dazzling white, anticipates the full manifestation of the kingdom of God that Jesus proclaimed. The Luminous Mysteries together help us to understand Jesus' identity which is always greater than we can comprehend.

Throughout the biblical tradition, certain places and motifs symbolize much more than earthly realities. From Sinai to Calvary, mountains are symbolic places of communication with the divine; clouds are signs of hope and of God's presence; white garments signify joy, celebration, and resurrected life; glory expresses the presence and splendor of God. The event on the mount of transfiguration, laden with such rich symbolism, gives us a momentary glimpse of Jesus in majesty, anticipating his eternal reign as the risen Lord.

Appearing with Jesus on the mountain are Moses and Elijah, great prophets of old who had experienced God's presence on a mountain, and who had suffered on account of their faithfulness to God. In Luke's Gospel, Jesus converses with them about the exodus which he is about to fulfill in Jerusalem. Recalling the exodus of the past, Jesus' own exodus will entail a passover from death to life in a journey marked by suffering and rejection. Even in the midst of the vision of radiant glory, the mystery of the cross cannot be escaped.

Peter, James and John, awakened from sleep, witness Jesus' transfiguration and see Moses and Elijah with him. As if to prolong the wondrous experience, Peter proposes building three tents, perhaps like those used at the harvest festival of Tabernacles. But rather than remaining on the mountain of glory, a voice from the cloud tells the awed disciples, "This is my Son, the beloved; listen to him" (Mark 9:7). The only command the three friends of Jesus receive is "Listen to him." They may not remain on the mountain, but must journey with Jesus to Jerusalem, listening to him as he teaches about discipleship and the cross and the coming exodus.

Even as the transfiguration of Jesus allows us to see him in majesty, we also get a hint of our own future transformation in him. As Saint Paul told the Corinthian community, although we now live in "earthen vessels" and are afflicted, God is preparing us for eternal glory exceeding all imagining (II Corinthians 4:7–18). While we reflect the glory of the Lord as in a mirror, God's own Spirit is transforming us into the very image that we reflect (II Corinthians 3:18). Even through we may not be able to see the mystery with our limited human vision, perceiving through a mirror only dimly, we are already being conformed to the very image of the risen Lord.

FOR REFLECTION

In the midst of Jesus' transfiguration, we speak of his exodus. Meditate on the entire process of Jesus' exodus/Passover leading to his glory.

How are you being transformed into the image of Christ?

The Fourth Luminous Mystery: The Transfiguration

The Fourth Luminous Mystery:
The Transfiguration

(STAND)

We saw his glory,
the glory as of the Father's only Son,
full of grace and truth.

(John 1:14)

Our Father

(SIT)

[Jesus] took Peter, John, and James…went up the mountain to pray.
While he was praying his face changed in appearance
and his clothing became dazzling white.

(Luke 9:28–29)

Hail Mary (3)

And behold, two men were conversing with him, Moses and Elijah,
who appeared in glory and spoke of his exodus
that he was going to accomplish in Jerusalem.

(Luke 9:30–31)

Hail Mary (3)

Peter and his companions had been overcome with sleep,
but becoming fully awake, they saw his glory
and the two men standing with him.

(Luke 9:32)

Hail Mary (3)

…a cloud came and cast a shadow over them,
and they became frightened when they entered the cloud.
Then from the cloud came a voice that said,
"This is my chosen Son; listen to him."

(Luke 9:34–35)

Hail Mary (1)

(STAND)

Glory to the Father

The Fifth Luminous Mystery:

CHRIST'S INSTITUTION OF THE EUCHARIST
Luke 22:14–28

It is an essential truth, not only of doctrine but also of life, that the Eucharist builds the Church, building it as the authentic community of the People of God, as the assembly of the faithful, bearing the same mark of unity that was shared by the Apostles and the first disciples of the Lord. The Eucharist builds ever anew this community and unity, ever building and regenerating it on the basis of the Sacrifice of Christ, since it commemorates his death on the Cross, the price by which he redeemed us.

Pope John Paul II,
Redeemer of Man
(Redemptor Hominis), 20

---

*P*assover is the annual feast of liberation and hope, a remembrance of God's past deliverance from slavery and confident anticipation of future deliverance. As we reflect on the Fifth Luminous Mystery, Christ's Institution of the Eucharist, we see Jesus eating a Passover meal with his disciples, celebrating together, remembering and giving thanks. Luke's Gospel, in which Jesus has already spoken of his coming exodus in Jerusalem, gives us the most detailed portrait of Jesus at this last Passover feast.

Before Jesus proceeds to the final stages of his exodus, he intensely desires to eat a Passover meal with his closest followers. The meal itself gives Jesus the perfect setting for explaining the sacrificial content of the suffering and death he is about to undergo. Using the symbols of the Passover meal, bread and a cup of wine, Jesus imbues them with new meaning. The bread is no longer just a symbol of past affliction, recalling the bread eaten in haste at the first Passover, but is Jesus' own body, broken and given to those he loves. The cup of wine is no longer just a reminder of the blood which sealed the covenant in the past and which protected the people from death, but is Jesus' own blood poured out in selfless love.

After giving his disciples the bread and wine, his very self, Jesus tells them "Do this in remembrance of me." When they "do this in remembrance," they repeat Jesus' actions of taking the bread and cup, giving thanks and dividing it among them. In so doing, even though Jesus will no longer be with them in the same way, they will be nourished by his continuing presence in the mystery of the bread and wine transformed.

The final meal with Jesus is the last of many Gospel scenes of table-fellowship and meal-sharing. The meal episodes illustrate the qualities the community is to manifest whenever and wherever they "do this" in his remembrance. Jesus ate with sinners and welcomed the outcast. Meals were occasions for offering forgiveness, for calling people to conversion of life, for exhorting those at table to act justly and to care for the poor. Taking on the role of servant himself, Jesus demonstrates that humble service is to be characteristic of table-fellowship. In the Last Supper scene in John's Gospel, Jesus, in a reversal of roles, washes his disciples' feet, giving them a model to follow. "Do this in remembrance of me."

When the community gathers in Jesus' name, he nourishes them both by his life-giving body and blood and by his life-giving word. At his final Passover celebration, Jesus instructed his disciples about the meaning of his own life and death, and explained to them their future responsibilities as disciples. As Jesus did in the upper room in Jerusalem, the church continues to do, nourishing the community through the proclamation of the word and through the sharing in the body and blood of the Lord. As community, we the living body of Christ, go forth from the eucharistic table to take what we have received as food for others. Repeating the pattern of Jesus' self-giving, by the power of his Spirit we "do this in remembrance of him."

FOR REFLECTION

"Eucharist" means "thanksgiving." Reflect on Jesus at the Last Supper, joining him in giving thanks for God's deliverance and mercy. Give thanks with the disciples for Jesus' gift of self in a new act of deliverance.

How do you "do this" in remembrance of Jesus?

· THE EUCHARIST ·

The Fifth Luminous Mystery: Christ's Institution of the Eucharist

The Fifth Luminous Mystery:
Christ's Institution of the Eucharist

(STAND)

Come, eat of my food,
and drink of the wine I have mixed!
(Proverbs 9:5)

Our Father

(SIT)

…the bread that I will give is my flesh for the life of the world.
(John 6:51c)

While they were eating, Jesus took bread, said the blessing, broke it,
and giving it to his disciples said: "Take and eat, this is my body."
(Matthew 26:26)

Hail Mary (3)

Then he took a cup, gave thanks, and gave it to them, saying,
"Drink from it, all of you, for this is my blood of the covenant,
which will be shed on behalf of many for the forgiveness of sins."
(Matthew 26:27)

Hail Mary (3)

[Jesus] rose from supper and took off his outer garments.
He took a towel and tied it around his waist. Then he poured water into a basin
and began to wash his disciples' feet and dry them with the towel around his waist.
(John 13:4–5)

Hail Mary (3)

"If I,…the master and teacher, have washed your feet,
you ought to wash one another's feet.
I have given you a model to follow,
so that as I have done for you, you should also do."
(John 13:14–15)

Hail Mary (1)

(STAND)

Glory to the Father

The First Sorrowful Mystery:

THE AGONY IN THE GARDEN
Matthew 26:36–46; Mark 14:32–42; Luke 22:39–46; John 18:1

The sequence of meditations begins with Gethsemane, where Christ experiences a moment of great anguish before the will of the Father, against which the weakness of the flesh would be tempted to rebel. There Jesus encounters all the temptations and confronts all the sins of humanity, in order to say to the Father: "Not my will but yours be done."

> Pope John Paul II,
> *The Rosary of the Virgin Mary*
> *(Rosarium Virginis Mariae)*, 22

Gethsemane on the Mount of Olives, a place familiar to Jesus and his disciples, is the setting for the First Sorrowful Mystery, the Agony in the Garden. Here we see Jesus, along with Peter, James and John, separated from the rest of his disciples for a time of prayer. The Twelve had often seen Jesus at prayer, and had asked that he teach them. Now in the garden, Jesus asks his closest followers, those who have learned from him both the words and the dispositions for prayer, to watch and to pray even as he had taught them, lest they be unable to withstand the time of testing to follow. Yet, from weakness of the flesh and anguish of spirit, the disciples repeatedly sleep through their appointed duty of prayer and keeping vigil. In the First Sorrowful Mystery, the disciples' sleeping highlights Jesus' isolation from human companionship and support, foreshadowing the abandonment that he will experience on the cross.

While the disciples are sleeping, Jesus prays intensely. Luke describes Jesus as being in *agonia*, a term which includes more than the English word "agony," with the added notion of struggle or contest, or even combat. Like an athlete, a person in *agonia* wrestles vigorously to attain victory. Thus had Jesus' ancestor Jacob wrestled with an angel throughout the night, ultimately prevailing. Here at Gethsemane, Jesus is likewise in an active struggle, wrestling against evil, darkness, and the piercing consciousness of the suffering he is about to undergo. As he is in *agonia*, Jesus prays ever more fervently, surely praying as he had taught his disciples to pray. He would speak to his Father with his own heartfelt words, as well as words from the prayers from his Jewish heritage.

The psalms especially would have come readily to Jesus' mind. From his childhood, he would have repeated the prayers so often that the familiar words would now resonate within him. In the midst of his *agonia*, Jesus would have joined his own prayer to the prayers of the poor, the captive, and the falsely accused who cried out their anguish to God in the psalms. The voices in the psalms declare over and over that God bestows kindness particularly on the lowly, as the mother of Jesus had proclaimed in her Magnificat (Luke 1:46–55). All the psalm pleas for mercy, compassion, and divine deliverance are expressions of confidence in the God who has the power and will to save.

As Jesus looks ahead to all he is still to endure, he asks his Father to act according to the pattern of deliverance exhibited in the psalms. He asks that God remove "this cup" from which Jesus will drink, a cup representing evil and suffering in all its dimensions. Even as he asks his Father to take away the cup of suffering, Jesus' stance is one of faithful obedience and absolute trust in God. Jesus' acceptance of his cup, choosing the Father's will over his own, echoes his mother's response at the annunciation. Mother and son alike say "yes" to whatever God's will may be for them, no matter the consequences, such that their own minds and wills are at one with the plan of God.

FOR REFLECTION

"Pray and keep vigil," Jesus tells his followers. How are you obedient to Jesus' bidding?

As you reflect on the Agony in the Garden, pray, along with Jesus, one or more Psalms of Lament, such as Psalm 13 or Psalm 25.

The First Sorrowful Mystery: The Agony in the Garden

The First Sorrowful Mystery:
The Agony in the Garden

(STAND)

My heart pounds within me;
death's terrors fall upon me.
Fear and trembling overwhelm me;
shuddering sweeps over me.

(Psalm 55:5–6)

Our Father

(SIT)

Then they came to a place named Gethsemane...
[Jesus] said to his disciples, "Sit here while I pray."
He took with him Peter, James, and John, and began to be troubled and distressed.
Then he said to them, "My soul is sorrowful even to death.
Remain here and keep watch."
He advanced a little and fell to the ground.

(Mark 14:32–34)

Hail Mary (3)

"My Father, if it is possible, let this cup pass from me;
yet not as I will, but as you will."

(Matthew 26:39b)

Hail Mary (3)

When he returned to his disciples he found them asleep.
He said to Peter, "So you could not keep watch with me for one hour?
Watch and pray that you may not undergo the test."

(Matthew 26:40–41)

Hail Mary (3)

He returned a third time and said to them,
"Are you still sleeping and taking your rest? It is enough.
The hour has come. Behold, the Son of Man is to be handed over to sinners.
Get up, let us go. See, my betrayer is at hand."

(Mark 14:41–42)

Hail Mary (1)

(STAND)

Glory to the Father

The Second Sorrowful Mystery:

THE SCOURGING AT THE PILLAR
Matthew 27:26; Mark 15:15; John 19:1

You know well enough that your ransom was not paid in earthly currency, silver or gold; it was paid in the precious blood of Christ; no lamb was ever so pure, so spotless a victim. If only they would lend a more eager ear to the apostle of the Gentiles: "A great price was paid to ransom you; glorify God by making your bodies the shrines of his presence."

Pope John XXIII,
On Promoting Devotion to the Most Precious
Blood of Our Lord Jesus Christ
(Sanguis Christi), 30 June 1960

---

*W*ith great brevity of language, in less than a sentence, the evangelists describe the scene of Jesus' being scourged by Pilate: "...after he had Jesus scourged, he handed him over..." (Matthew 27:26; Mark 15:15). The Third Sorrowful Mystery, the Scourging at the Pillar, so starkly stated, emphasizes the harshness and injustice inflicted on Jesus.

Prior to Jesus' scourging, the Roman governor Pontius Pilate directs sharp questions both at Jesus and at the crowd. Pilate's questions, growing ever more intense throughout the scene, point to the shock and bewilderment surrounding the events of Jesus' Passion. Pilate asks Jesus if he is the King of the Jews and if he has no answer to make to the charges against him. Only in John's Gospel does Jesus answer directly. He says that his kingship is not "of this world," and that the very purpose of his birth is to "bear witness to the truth." Pilate, though puzzled by Jesus' words, can find no reason to condemn him.

Having found Jesus to be blameless, Pilate turns his questioning to the crowd. Do they want Pilate to release Jesus the King of the Jews or Barabbas the insurrectionist? The cry for Barabbas' release leads Pilate to ask further, "What shall I do with this man?" When the crowd shouts "Crucify him!" Pilate asks his final, most baffled, question, "Why, what evil has he done?" No answer except, "Crucify him!" And the urgent demanding of the crowd prevails.

Thus Pilate, even though his own questioning had led him to recognize Jesus' innocence, orders that Jesus be flogged, the humiliating and harsh punishment inflicted on slaves and provincials sentenced to death. Carried out with metal and bone-studded whips, scourging weakened those about to be executed. At this moment, we hear no words from Jesus or Pilate or the crowds. The very brevity of description keeps focus centered on Jesus as he drinks from the cup of suffering.

Having scourged Jesus, Pilate hands him over to be crucified.

The Gospel accounts of Pilate's questioning and Jesus' scourging are reminiscent of Isaiah the prophet's description of the righteous suffering servant. The servant in Isaiah is despised, abject, acquainted with infirmity, and considered of no account. His wounds and bruising are endured for our iniquities and for our sins. And in the torment of suffering, the servant remains silent (Isaiah 53:3–7). Whatever Isaiah's original understanding may have been, Jesus in his Passion remarkably mirrors the depiction of God's servant whose unwavering fidelity brings salvation even to those who persecute him. Jesus, the righteous servant of God, continues the path that leads him ultimately to Calvary.

FOR REFLECTION

Reflect on Jesus' silence as he is scourged. What words do you imagine Jesus speaking to his Father?

How do you pray when you are suffering?

The Second Sorrowful Mystery: The Scourging at the Pillar

The Second Sorrowful Mystery:
The Scourging at the Pillar

(STAND)

Upon him was the chastisement that makes us whole,
by his stripes we were healed.

(Isaiah 53:5b)

Our Father

(SIT)

Like a lamb led to the slaughter
or a sheep before the shearers,
he was silent and opened not his mouth.

(Isaiah 53:7b)

When it was morning....They bound him, led him away,
and handed him over to Pilate...[who] questioned him,
"Are you the king of the Jews?" Jesus said: "You say so."

(Matthew 27:1, 2; 11)

Hail Mary (3)

Then Pilate said to him,
"Do you not hear how many things they are testifying against you?"
But he did not answer him one word, so that the governor was greatly amazed.

(Matthew 27:13–14)

Hail Mary (3)

[Pilate said to the crowd]: "Which of the two do you want me to release to you?"
They answered "Barabbas!" Pilate said to them,
"Then what shall I do with Jesus called the Messiah?"
They all said, "Let him be crucified!"

(Matthew 27:21–22)

Hail Mary (3)

So Pilate, wishing to satisfy the crowd,
released Barabbas to them and,
after he had Jesus scourged, handed him over to be crucified.

(Mark 15:15)

Hail Mary (1)

(STAND)

Glory to the Father

The Third Sorrowful Mystery:

THE CROWNING WITH THORNS
Matthew 27:27–31; Mark 15:17–20; John 19:2–15

Christ drew close above all to the world of human suffering through the fact of having taken this suffering upon his very self. During his public activity, he experienced not only fatigue, homelessness, misunderstanding even on the part of those closest to him, but, more than anything, he became progressively more and more isolated and encircled by hostility and the preparations for putting him to death.

Pope John Paul II,
The Christian Meaning of Suffering
(Salvifici Doloris), 16

———————————

*T*hroughout his ministry Jesus proclaimed the good news of the kingdom of God, present in his very person and unfolding mysteriously like growing seeds. The kingdom that he announces is one of forgiveness and love, a kingdom that welcomes sinners and shows compassion on the unloved. In the Third Sorrowful Mystery, the Crowning with Thorns, the meaning of the kingdom of God is twisted and distorted and ridiculed.

After Jesus' scourging, the soldiers subject him to one humiliating insult after another, all of them mocking his kingship. They strip him; they robe him in a cloak of regal purple; they press a crown of woven thorns onto his head; and after they put a reed for a scepter in his hand, they salute him with derision, "Hail, King of the Jews." They spit on him, strike him, and kneel before him in taunting homage. All of the actions and words in this scene are inflicted upon Jesus. From Jesus himself, we hear no speech and see no movement. Like the suffering servant in Isaiah (Isaiah 50:6), Jesus does not shield himself from the beating, buffets, and spitting of his tormentors.

Little do the soldiers realize that in their mocking, they have correctly identified Jesus. He is a king. Although the soldiers use cloak, crown, and scepter, symbols of earthly kingship, Jesus' kingdom is not of this world. The meaning of his kingship that transcends earthly rule is most fully developed in the dialogue between Jesus and Pilate as presented in John's Gospel. Pilate declares that he has power either to release or to crucify Jesus. To Pilate's blustering boast, Jesus replies that the only power Pilate has comes "from above." Pilate's apparent authority falls before the ultimate authority that comes from above.

Jesus' reply to Pilate evokes an earlier scene in John's Gospel in which Jesus explains to Nicodemus that only those born from above are able to see the kingdom of God (John 3:3). Whether for Nicodemus or Pilate or ourselves, only God's power from above can bring about recognition of Jesus as king. Pilate, afraid of the crowds and protective of his shaky power, remains blind to Jesus' kingly identity. He presents Jesus to the crowd saying, "Behold your king!" and asks a final ironic question, "Shall I crucify your king?" Because the chief priests insist that they have no king but Caesar, the fearful Pilate hands Jesus over to be crucified.

Jesus' crowning with thorns and all the symbolic ridicule of his regal status highlight the contrast between appearances and reality. Appearing as lowly and powerless, Jesus is in reality the kingly son of God. The apparent political authority of Pilate is in reality subject to God's power from above. While Pilate appears to be in charge of the proceedings, in reality he gives in to the will of the people; Jesus, on the other hand, does only the will of his Father. And the handing over of Jesus to crucifixion, the apparent end of his false messianic claims, leads in reality to the beginning of his eternal reign.

FOR REFLECTION

What does it mean to you that Jesus is a king? How does he exercise kingly power?

What things assist you in seeing beyond appearances to deeper realities? What things prevent you?

·THE CROWNING WITH THORNS·

The Third Sorrowful Mystery: The Crowning with Thorns

The Third Sorrowful Mystery:
The Crowning with Thorns

(STAND)

I gave my back to those who beat me,
my cheeks to those who plucked my beard;
My face I did not shield
from buffets and spitting.

(Isaiah 50:6)

Our Father

(SIT)

All who see me mock me;
they curl their lips and jeer;...
"You relied on the LORD...
if he loves you, let him rescue you."

(Psalm 22:8–9)

Hail Mary (3)

[The soldiers] stripped off his clothes and threw a scarlet military cloak about him.
Weaving a crown out of thorns, they placed it on his head,
and a reed in his right hand.

(Matthew 27:28–29a)

Hail Mary (3)

And kneeling before him, they mocked him, saying,
"Hail, King of the Jews!"
They spat upon him and took the reed
and kept striking him on the head.

(Matthew 27:29b–30)

Hail Mary (3)

And when they had mocked him, they stripped him of the cloak,
dressed him in his own clothes, and led him off to crucify him.

(Matthew 27:31)

Hail Mary (1)

(STAND)

Glory to the Father

The Fourth Sorrowful Mystery:

THE CARRYING OF THE CROSS
Matthew 27:32–34; Mark 15:20–21; Luke 23:26–32; John 19:17

He gave us His new commandment to love one another as He loved us. He taught us the way of the beatitudes of the Gospel: poverty in spirit, meekness, suffering borne with patience, thirst after justice, mercy, purity of heart, will for peace, persecution suffered for justice sake. Under Pontius Pilate He suffered—the Lamb of God bearing on Himself the sins of the world, and He died for us on the cross, saving us by His redeeming blood.

Pope Paul VI,
The Credo of the People of God
(Sollemni Hac Liturgia),
30 June 1968

---

*J*esus, scourged and mocked, has already been punished with the harshness reserved for slaves and non-Roman citizens, their ultimate punishment being death by crucifixion. In the Fourth Sorrowful Mystery, the Carrying of the Cross, Jesus, treated as the lowliest of slaves, bears upon his shoulders the instrument of his own execution. The cross that he carries is also a tangible sign that Jesus, the suffering servant, bears the weight of our infirmities.

Each of the Gospel-writers offers different details about Jesus' road to Calvary. John, most briefly, tells us that Jesus himself carried the cross, whereas the other Evangelists say that Simon of Cyrene was compelled to bear the cross behind Jesus. The accounts together present an image of Jesus, already weakened from the scourging, bearing his cross alone as long as he is able, and at the end being assisted by Simon. Although Simon's appearance is brief, we see him as the first person to comply with Jesus' command to take up the cross and follow him (Matthew 16:24), thereby becoming a model of discipleship.

For the Roman soldiers, Jesus is simply another condemned criminal and the road to his execution of no consequence. However, as Jesus makes his way to the Place of the Skull (Golgotha), multitudes follow him, including some women who are weeping and lamenting (Luke 23:28). Whether disciples of Jesus or women of the city mourning an unjust execution, these women show courage and compassion in speaking to the condemned man. Their grieving stands in sharp contrast with the exuberant rejoicing of the multitudes just a few days earlier when Jesus entered the city. Jesus, who had uttered so few words throughout his Passion, now turns to the women, addressing them with prophetic words. As he somberly predicts the violence that will fall upon even the innocent, he urges the women to weep for themselves and their children. Although Jesus is speaking specifically about the fate of Jerusalem, his words also remind us that wherever injustices and violence are inflicted, there is cause for mourning, for their effects strike down on the innocent and vulnerable.

The road traveled by Jesus, Simon, and the crowds who follow is a continuation of the path on which Jesus had already been proceeding. After preaching and teaching and healing in Galilee, Jesus resolutely set out for Jerusalem. Nothing deterred him from taking the road which would assuredly lead to Calvary. Even when he is warned not to go up to the holy city, Jesus continues to go forward. He is undeterred in completing his journey.

As he made his way to Jerusalem, Jesus taught those closest to him how to be his disciples. He demonstrated both by his prophetic words and by his actions that the disciples traveling with him must follow the same path—one marked by suffering and rejection. Like Jesus, all of the men and women who follow him on the way must deny themselves, bear the crosses they are given, and be servants to one another. Like Simon of Cyrene, disciples share the burdens of those unable to carry their crosses alone. And, like Jesus, they must complete the journey, following the path that Jesus walked.

FOR REFLECTION

What does the cross that Jesus carries symbolize for you?

What are the burdens that you are asked to carry? Whom do you assist in bearing the cross?

The Fourth Sorrowful Mystery: The Carrying of the Cross

The Fourth Sorrowful Mystery:
The Carrying of the Cross

(STAND)

...it was our infirmities that he bore,
our sufferings that he endured.

(Isaiah 53:4a)

Our Father

(SIT)

So they took Jesus, and carrying the cross himself,
he went out to what is called the Place of the Skull,
in Hebrew, Golgotha.

(John 19:16b–17)

Hail Mary (3)

...I will lay down my life for the sheep....No one takes it from me,
but I lay it down on my own. I have power to lay it down,
and power to take it up again.

(John 10:15b, 18)

Hail Mary (3)

Whoever wishes to come after me must deny himself,
take up his cross and follow me.

(Mark 8:34)

Hail Mary (3)

As they led him away they took hold of a certain Simon, a Cyrenian...and after
laying the cross on him, they made him carry it behind Jesus.

(Luke 23:26)

Hail Mary (1)

(STAND)

Glory to the Father

The Fifth Sorrowful Mystery:

THE CRUCIFIXION
Luke 23:32–49; John 19:23–30

The sorrowful mysteries help the believer to relive the death of Jesus, to stand at the foot of the Cross beside Mary, to enter with her into the depths of God's love for man and to experience all its life-giving power.

Pope John Paul II,
The Rosary of the Virgin Mary
(Rosarium Virginis Mariae), 22

———————

*F*rom the agony in Gethsemane, to the scourging and crowning with thorns, the mocking and condemnation, and on the road to Golgotha, Jesus radiated strength and authority even in the face of escalating abuse. Physically weakened though he was, he manifest a kingship "not of this world" and relied on power "from above." In the final hours of his life, Jesus on the cross reveals most fully the meaning of his kingship and the source of his power. Each Gospel writer illuminates different dimensions of the Fifth Sorrowful Mystery, the Crucifixion.

The account of Jesus' crucifixion in Mark's Gospel, closely followed by Matthew, is remarkably concise and focused. Brief as the narrative is, Mark says three times, "they crucified him," drawing our attention to Jesus alone on the cross, abandoned by all his disciples except a few women. From this cross, Jesus cries out in agony, "My God, my God, why have you abandoned me?" As Jesus breathes out his last, the curtain of the temple is ripped in two, reminiscent of the ripping of the heavens at Jesus' baptism. The rending of the heavens and of the temple curtain each signal an end of the separation between God and humanity. At the same moment, the Roman centurion declares that Jesus is Son of God, becoming the first human person to proclaim Jesus' true identity.

Throughout Mark's account, he alludes to Psalm 22, a lament of an innocent person who suffers at the hands of persecutors and is ultimately delivered by God. The dividing of Jesus' garments and casting lots for them, the mockery and shaking of heads are all details found in Psalm 22. Jesus' final cry from the cross is taken from the opening words of this psalm. In the context of Psalm 22, Jesus expresses both the depth of his suffering and his confidence in God's power to rescue him. Use of Psalm 22 and other allusions to the Hebrew Scriptures remind us also that Jesus' Passion and death happened "according to the Scriptures."

Luke's portrait of Jesus on the cross fills out that of Mark. In Luke's Gospel, from the first words that Jesus speaks as a twelve-year old in the Temple, he is involved in the concerns of his Father. On the cross, Jesus continues his mission in union with his

Father. He asks his Father to forgive those who do not know what they are doing, promises paradise to the thief, and confidently commits his Spirit into his Father's hands. Jesus' death on the cross, like his entire life, manifests his intimate communion with his Father and the unwavering love of Father and Son toward sinners and the outcast.

In John's Gospel, the crucifixion of Jesus is the hour in which, having loved his own to the end, Jesus passes from this world to the Father. In the hour of Jesus' Passion, we see him as king even on the cross. There the title "king of the Jews," written in three languages to announce Jesus' false kingly claims to everyone, becomes instead a universal proclamation of his true kingly identity. Jesus' mother stands by the cross, accompanied by other faithful women and the beloved disciple. His mother had been with Jesus at Cana before his hour had come, and now she remains courageously at the hour of his dying. In this scene, we see her first as a mother witnessing with anguish the unjust violence directed against her son. We see her also, in company with the beloved disciple to whom Jesus entrusted her, as representative of the new family created by her son's sacrifice on the cross.

The cross of Christ is an instrument of harsh punishment and a mark of repudiation. This cross is transformed by the total self-giving of the Son of God, becoming a sign of God's communion with us, the place of forgiveness and mercy, a symbol of love and hope and of new creation.

FOR REFLECTION

Pray Psalm 22, contemplating the image of Jesus as the innocent, suffering, and vindicated righteous man.

What words or images come to mind when you think of the cross of Christ? Ponder the meaning of each of these.

The Fifth Sorrowful Mystery: The Crucifixion

The Fifth Sorrowful Mystery:
The Crucifixion

(STAND)

…when I am lifted up from the earth, I will draw everyone to myself.

(John 12:32)

Our Father

(SIT)

We proclaim Christ crucified, a stumbling block and foolishness.
We proclaim Christ crucified, the wisdom of God.

(based on 1 Corinthians 1:23–24)

…they crucified him and the criminals there, one on his right, the other on his left.
[Then Jesus said, "Father, forgive them, they know not what they do."]
They divided his garments by casting lots.

(Luke 23:33–34)

Hail Mary (3)

So wasted are my hands and feet
that I can count all my bones.
…they divide my garments among them;
for my clothing they cast lots.

(Psalm 22:17b, 18a, 19)

Hail Mary (3)

Standing by the cross of Jesus were his mother
and his mother's sister, Mary the wife of Cleopas, and Mary of Magdala.
When Jesus saw his mother and the disciple there whom he loved,
he said to his mother, "Woman, behold, your son."
Then he said to the disciple, "Behold, your mother."
And from that hour the disciple took her into his home.

(John 19:25–27)

Hail Mary (3)

Jesus cried out in a loud voice,
"Father, into your hands I commend my spirit";
and when he had said this he breathed his last.

(Luke 23:46)

Hail Mary (1)

(STAND)

Glory to the Father

The First Glorious Mystery:

THE RESURRECTION
Luke 24:1–35; John 20:1–28

> In the Liturgy of [Easter] we hear the announcement: "Our Lord Jesus Christ, after His resurrection, stood in the midst of His disciples and said 'Peace be to you,' alleluia: the disciples rejoiced seeing the Lord." He leaves us peace, He brings us peace: "Peace I leave with you, my peace I give to you; not as the world gives do I give to you."
>
> Pope John XXIII,
> *Peace on Earth*
> *(Pacem in Terris)*, 170

---

*A*n empty tomb and a young man in a white robe saying, "He is not here." There are the linen cloths and wrappings, but no sign of Jesus. The experience of the women at the tomb is one of absence. However, the First Glorious Mystery, the Resurrection, is about presence—the new and abiding presence of the Risen One.

Reacting with emotions ranging from fear to great joy, the women at the tomb hurriedly tell the other disciples what they have seen and heard. Many of the disciples appear sad and discouraged at the loss of Jesus. We see this in the weeping of Mary Magdalene, the dejection of the two disciples on the road to Emmaus, and the doubting of Thomas. For each of them, an unexpected encounter with the risen Jesus transforms their sadness into joy and their doubt into faith.

When the risen Jesus appears to Mary Magdalene, she does not recognize him, thinking him to be a gardener. With great gentleness, Jesus reveals his identity to her, addressing her simply by her name, "Mary." She knows immediately who is speaking to her, and responds just as simply, "Rabboni." Similarly, the disciples trudging to Emmaus do not recognize Jesus, seeing him as just a stranger on the road. Only after he explains the Scriptures and breaks the bread with them are their eyes opened and do their hearts burn within them. In another appearance, Jesus leads the skeptical Thomas to recognition and faith by inviting him to touch the visible marks of the wounds in his hands and side, changing Thomas' disbelief to belief.

When they recognize the risen Jesus present with them, Mary Magdalene, the two disciples, and Thomas all become bearers of the good news. Mary becomes the first to announce the resurrection, proclaiming, "I have seen the Lord." The two Emmaus-bound disciples, having abandoned the community, return saying they recognized Jesus in the breaking of the bread. And Thomas, at first refusing to believe that Jesus had risen, acknowledges him as "My Lord and my God."

Jesus appears also to the gathered but fearful community of disciples, greeting them with a proclamation of peace. His words are more than a standard greeting, for Jesus had told his disciples at their last meal that peace was his gift to them. The peace that he imparts drives out their fear and will accompany them when they go forth to continue his mission of bringing the good news.

One of the few words from the Hebrew Scriptures that remains untranslated in English is *alleluia*, which means "praise the Lord." Alleluia is a word that extols the God who came to be known in the deeds of creating, redeeming, and teaching the people. In the resurrection of Jesus, the alleluias and acclamations of the biblical tradition have a new meaning! Our alleluias express amazement and awe because of the abundant manifestations of God's love and mercy in raising Jesus from the dead. In the risen Lord Jesus, God continues to redeem, gather, feed, and teach the people. Like the first disciples who experienced the risen Lord, we, too, hear his words spoken to us, share in the breaking of bread with him, and receive his gift of peace. Let us join the first believers in taking the good news of Jesus' resurrection as a source of life, light, and joy for the world. The Lord Jesus is risen! Alleluia!

FOR REFLECTION

The risen Jesus is present among us. Reflect on how and where you recognize him.

How do you experience Jesus' gift of peace and extend that peace to others?

The First Glorious Mystery: The Resurrection

The First Glorious Mystery:
The Resurrection

(STAND)

All who call upon me I will answer;
I will be with them in distress;
I will deliver them and give them honor.

(Psalm 91:15)

Our Father

(SIT)

At daybreak on the first day of the week
[the women]…took the spices…and went to the tomb.
They found the stone rolled away from the tomb;
but…they did not find the body of the Lord Jesus.
While they were puzzling over this, behold,
two men in dazzling garments appeared to them.…They said to them:
"Why do you seek the living among the dead?
He is not here, but he has been raised."

(Luke 24:1–6a)

Hail Mary (3)

"Remember what he said to you while he was still in Galilee,
that the Son of Man must be handed over to sinners and be crucified,
and rise on the third day." And they remembered his words.

(Luke 24:6b–8)

Hail Mary (3)

Then they returned from the tomb
and announced all these things to the eleven and to all the others.
…but their story seemed like nonsense and they did not believe them.

(Luke 24:9–11)

Hail Mary (3)

But Peter got up and ran to the tomb,
bent down, and saw the burial clothes alone;
then he went home amazed at what had happened.

(Luke 24:12)

Hail Mary (1)

(STAND)

Glory to the Father

The Second Glorious Mystery:

THE ASCENSION
Matthew 28:16–20; Luke 24:44–53; Acts of the Apostles 1:6–11

All the Evangelists, when they describe the risen Christ's meeting with his apostles, conclude with the "missionary mandate…The different versions of the "missionary mandate" contain common elements as well as characteristics proper to each. Two elements, however, are found in all the versions. First, there is the universal dimension of the task entrusted to the apostles, who are sent to "all nations" (Matthew 28:19)…Secondly, there is the assurance given to the Apostles by the Lord that they will not be alone in the task, but will receive the strength and the means necessary to carry out their mission.

Pope John Paul II,
On the Permanent Validity of the
Church's Missionary Mandate
(Redemptoris Missio), 22–23

---

*B*efore the risen Jesus ascends to his Father, he meets with the eleven apostles a final time, giving them both a commissioning and a promise. In the Second Glorious Mystery, the Ascension, our reflection on Jesus ascending into the heavens moves us to look back on his entire mission on earth and to look forward to his continuing presence in the life of the church.

In Matthew's Gospel, when Jesus speaks to his disciples for the last time, he tells them that they are to go forth and make disciples, baptizing and teaching all nations to obey all that Jesus commanded. Those gathered around Jesus have already become disciples, and now they are to make disciples, not only of their own people, but of all nations of the world. Looking back on the whole of the Gospel, we see how Jesus formed his small group of diverse and often uncomprehending followers into disciples. First he called them, and then he taught them, combining the Jewish traditions with his new instruction, teaching by word and example. In all that he did, Jesus embodied the very presence of God, for he was identified even at his birth as Emmanuel, God-with-us. Before he ascends, Jesus promises that he will continue to be present among his disciples even to the end of the ages. As we look beyond the ascension, we see Jesus' abiding presence in the church as the community of disciples continues to teach in the pattern of Jesus. He remains present where two or three disciples are gathered in his name, present in word and sacrament, and present in the least of our brothers and sisters.

Luke tells the story of Jesus' ascension twice, first at the end of his Gospel and then at the beginning of his second volume, the Acts of the Apostles. The twice-told event enables Luke to emphasize the link between the story of Jesus and the story of the church, again directing our attention both to the past and to the future. Before he ascends, Jesus reminds his disciples that they must remember the accounts of God's saving deeds in the past in order to comprehend God's action in Jesus. The Hebrew Scriptures prepared the way for Jesus, and are brought to fulfillment in him. As he opens the minds of the disciples to understand the Scriptures, Jesus explains that the sacred writings also give direction for the future. The mission of taking the good news to all the nations continues God's ancient plan of bringing salvation to the ends of the earth, already announced in the Law, the Psalms and the Prophets. Beginning in Jerusalem, Jesus' followers are to preach repentance and forgiveness in his name to all peoples. The Holy Spirit, the promised gift of God, will empower Jesus' followers to carry out their mission, and to be his witnesses to the ends of the earth.

Jesus' ascension into the heavens culminates his *exodus* by which he passes from this world and returns to his Father. The risen Jesus, having ascended into glory, is now seated at the right hand of God. After his ascension, although Jesus is no longer physically present, he continues to be a central participant in the story of his followers. He is the one awaited from heaven; he is the resurrected one to whom the church bears witness; he is the exalted one who, with the Father, sends forth the Spirit. Jesus continues to be God-with-us, ever faithful to his promises, and gives us the gifts we need to continue his mission.

FOR REFLECTION

Since Jesus has ascended into heaven, we await his return. How?

Pray to Jesus as the ascended, exalted Lord. How does speaking to him from this perspective affect your prayer?

The Second Glorious Mystery: The Ascension

The Second Glorious Mystery:
The Ascension

(STAND)

See, my servant shall prosper,
he shall be raised on high and greatly exalted.

(Isaiah 52:13)

Our Father

(SIT)

He led them [out] as far as Bethany, raised his hands, and blessed them.
As he blessed them he parted from them and was taken up to heaven.

(Luke 24:50–51)

Hail Mary (3)

[After Jesus had been taken up to heaven the apostles] returned to Jerusalem
from the mount called Olivet, which is near Jerusalem, a sabbath day's journey away.
When they entered the city they went to the upper room where they were staying...

(Acts of the Apostles 1:12–13a)

Hail Mary (3)

All these devoted themselves with one accord to prayer,
together with some women, and Mary the mother of Jesus, and his brothers.

(Acts of the Apostles 1:14)

Hail Mary (3)

[Before he was taken up, Jesus] enjoined them...to wait
for "the promise of the Father about which you have heard me speak;
for John baptized with water, but in a few days
you will be baptized with the holy Spirit."

(Acts of the Apostles 1:4–5)

Hail Mary (1)

(STAND)

Glory to the Father

The Third Glorious Mystery:
THE DESCENT OF THE HOLY SPIRIT
Acts of the Apostles 2:1–42

After the resurrection and ascension of Jesus, the apostles have a powerful experience which completely transforms them: the experience of Pentecost. The coming of the Holy Spirit makes them *witnesses* and *prophets* (cf. Acts of the Apostles 1:8; 2:17–18). It fills them with a serene courage which impels them to pass on to others their experience of Jesus and the hope which motivates them. The Spirit gives them the ability to bear witness to Jesus with "boldness."

Pope John Paul II,
On the Permanent Validity of the
Church's Missionary Mandate
(Redemptoris Missio), 24

*S*acred Scripture tells repeatedly of God's promises given and promises brought to fulfillment. Fulfillment of promises shows God fidelity and assures that promises not-yet-fulfilled will ultimately be accomplished. The Third Glorious Mystery, the Descent of the Holy Spirit, is a powerful and dramatic manifestation of promises fulfilled and new promise given. God's promise of pouring out the Spirit on all flesh, and Jesus' promise of sending the Holy Spirit on his disciples are fulfilled at Pentecost; and the Holy Spirit is God's new promise of continuing guidance of the church born at Pentecost.

After Jesus ascends into heaven, his disciples gather in the upper room where they remain faithfully united in prayer. Included in the group are the apostles, Jesus' mother Mary, and other women and men, one hundred twenty in all. With other Jewish pilgrims, the disciples of Jesus were in Jerusalem to celebrate Pentecost, an annual feast for giving thanks for the harvest and renewing the covenant made on Mount Sinai. As wind and fire and trumpet blast had announced divine power and presence when the covenant was made at Sinai, now the sound as of a mighty wind and the appearance of tongues as of fire again show forth God's power and presence. And as God had formed a people by the covenant at Sinai, a new people is formed by the Pentecost event.

At Pentecost, the rushing wind and fire are manifestations of the outpouring of the Holy Spirit, the very breath of God who infuses life into this newly created community. The tongues given by the Spirit empower each member of the community to proclaim the mighty deeds of God for all to hear. The languages spoken by the Spirit-filled community are intelligible and unifying, unlike the languages at the tower of

Babel which had confused and divided the peoples of the earth. Thus promises fulfilled bring about a reversal of long-standing alienation, and engender hope that the experience of Pentecost will ultimately embrace all the peoples of the world.

As spokesman for the Spirit-filled community, Peter addresses the assembled crowd. His sermon interprets the event they have experienced, explaining that what they have seen and heard fulfills God's promise of pouring out the Spirit on all flesh, as foretold by the prophet Joel. Then, in Spirit-inspired prophetic language, Peter preaches Jesus crucified, raised and exalted, seated at the right hand of God, and now proclaimed both Lord and Christ. In his preaching, Peter imparts more than information to his audience, for they are cut to the heart by his words, and ask what they are to do. Peter's answer is clear and direct. They are to repent and be baptized, and they also will receive the Holy Spirit. The power of the Spirit given first to the one hundred twenty disciples now extends to three thousand more, a sign of promise fulfilled and a seed of new promise, assuring that those still far off will also receive God's Spirit.

The Holy Spirit, gift and promise of God, remains the life-sustaining breath of the church beyond Pentecost. By the power of the Holy Spirit, the earliest believers remained faithful to the teaching of the apostles, to communion with God and one another, to the breaking of the bread and the prayers. The Spirit gave them the courage to proclaim Jesus even when they faced persecution and martyrdom. The Holy Spirit is promise fulfilled, and promise given anew to each person baptized into Christ, empowering each one of us to continue the life and mission inaugurated at Pentecost.

———————————

FOR REFLECTION

What signs do you see that the Spirit who descended at Pentecost is still guiding the church?

How do you (individually and as communities), remain faithful to the teaching of the apostles, Communion, the breaking of the bread, and the prayers?

The Third Glorious Mystery: The Descent of the Holy Spirit

The Third Glorious Mystery:
The Descent of the Holy Spirit

(STAND)

I will put my spirit in you that you may live.

(Ezekiel 37:14)

Our Father

(SIT)

When the time for Pentecost was fulfilled, they were all in one place together.
And suddenly there came from the sky a noise like a strong driving wind,
and it filled the entire house in which they were.

(Acts of the Apostles 2:1–2)

Hail Mary (3)

Then there appeared to them tongues as of fire,
which parted and came to rest on each of them.
And they were all filled with the holy Spirit and began to
speak in different tongues, as the Spirit enabled them to proclaim.

(Acts of the Apostles 2:3–4)

Hail Mary (3)

Are not all these people who are speaking Galileans?
…yet we hear them speaking in our own tongues of the mighty acts of God.

(Acts of the Apostles 2:7b–8, 11b)

Hail Mary (3)

This is how we know that we remain in him and he in us,
that he has given us of his Spirit.

(1 John 4:13)

Hail Mary (1)

(STAND)

Glory to the Father

The Fourth Glorious Mystery:

THE ASSUMPTION

The solemnity of August 15 celebrates the glorious Assumption of Mary into heaven. It is a feast of her destiny of fullness and blessedness, of the glorification of her immaculate soul and of her virginal body, of her perfect configuration to the Risen Christ, a feast that sets before the eyes of the Church and of all mankind the image and the consoling proof of the fulfillment of their final hope, namely, that this full glorification is the destiny of all those whom Christ has made His brothers, having "flesh and blood in common with them" (Hebrews 2:14; cf. Galatians 4:4).

Pope Paul VI,
*On the Right Ordering and Development of
Devotion to the Blessed Virgin Mary
(Marialis Cultus),* 6

---

*T*he Descent of the Holy Spirit reveals divine promises fulfilled and generates hope for future accomplishment of all God's promises. In a like manner, the Fourth Glorious Mystery, the Assumption, is both promise fulfilled and a sign of hope for fulfillment of future divine deeds. God's saving action in Mary is a promise of what God has in store for us on our pilgrim way.

In her Magnificat of praise (Luke 1:46–55), Mary rejoices that God, who has done great things for her, extends mercy from generation to generation. Mary's prayer has a timeless quality about it, for her declarations about God's saving actions embrace past, present, and future. Her proclamation that God exalts the lowly ones has already been accomplished in God's past deeds of freeing an enslaved people and making a covenant with them. God's exaltation of the lowly is brought about in Mary's own day when she, a lowly maidservant, is chosen to be mother of the Messiah. Her joyful proclamation is also a prophetic promise that future generations will experience again God's exalting of the lowly. By assuming Mary into heavenly glory, God has exalted the lowly in a singular fashion. The humble woman of Nazareth, who had been united with her son in perfect fidelity to God's will, is now united with him in eternal life, exalted to the heavens. The life-long union Mary shared with her son on earth is continued in eternity.

The church, both in prayer and in official pronouncements, has frequently spoken of the unique privileges God has granted Mary. She alone is conceived without sin. She alone bears the Messiah. She alone gives birth while remaining a virgin. She alone represents the whole church as she stands at the foot of the cross. Mary's assumption into heaven, whereby God grants her another unique gift of even now sharing eternal life in fullness, is a further privilege fitting for the mother of God.

Though hers is a unique privilege, Mary's assumption is also a promise of what has been prepared for those who love God. The perishable body will become imperishable and the mortal will become immortal. Mary's assumption into heaven anticipates the eternal blessedness promised to all the lowly ones whom God will exalt. As she was united with the community at Pentecost, praying and receiving the Holy Spirit with them, Mary will be united with them in glory. Mary is an image of the church, and her assumption is the beginning and pattern of the church, a sure sign of hope and comfort.

Celebration of Mary's assumption and reflection on this mystery is not centered on a past event. As we remember God's gracious action of taking Mary into heaven, we give thanks that the mother of the church even now shows us our final destiny. Moreover, her bodily assumption helps us to value the dignity of the human body which is made to share in the glory of heaven. Her assumption into eternal life, a promise of what awaits us, counteracts pessimism and despair, replacing it with a firmly grounded hope. The longings we have for communion and wholeness will be satisfied when our lowly bodies, too, are exalted in fulfillment of God's promise, already begun in Mary's assumption.

FOR REFLECTION

Mary is unique and yet one of us. How do you see Mary as an integral member of the Communion of Saints?

The Assumption of Mary is a feast of hope. Reflect on what this means for you.

The Fourth Glorious Mystery: The Assumption

The Fourth Glorious Mystery:
The Assumption

(STAND)

Come and hear, all you who fear God,
while I recount what he has done for me.
(Psalm 66:16)

Our Father

(SIT)

My soul proclaims the greatness of the Lord;
my spirit rejoices in God my savior.
For he has looked upon his handmaid's lowliness;
behold, from now on will all ages call me blessed.
(Luke 1:46–48)

Hail Mary (3)

The Mighty One has done great things for me,
and holy is his name.
His mercy is from age to age
to those who fear him.
He has shown might with his arm,
dispersed the arrogant of mind and heart.
(Luke 1:49–51)

Hail Mary (3)

He has thrown down the rulers from their thrones
but lifted up the lowly.
The hungry he has filled with good things;
the rich he has sent away empty.
(Luke 1:52–53)

Hail Mary (3)

He has helped Israel his servant,
remembering his mercy,
according to his promise to our fathers,
to Abraham and his descendants forever.
(Luke 1:54–55)

Hail Mary (1)

(STAND)

Glory to the Father

The Fifth Glorious Mystery:

THE CORONATION

The Solemnity of the Assumption is prolonged in the celebration of the
Queenship of the Blessed Virgin Mary, which occurs seven days later. On this
occasion we contemplate her who, seated beside the King of ages, shines
forth as Queen and intercedes as Mother.

Pope Paul VI,
On the Right Ordering and Development of
Devotion to the Blessed Virgin Mary
(Marialis Cultus), 6

*A*n array of titles and images honoring Mary express her preeminent place in
the divine plan. Over and over we address her as Queen: Queen of prophets,
Queen of apostles, martyrs, and confessors, Queen of all saints, Queen of
peace. We sing the Easter antiphon "Queen of heaven rejoice alleluia!" In the Fifth
Glorious Mystery, the Coronation, we reflect on Mary, exalted by God as Queen in
heaven.

Reflection on biblical texts provide an entryway onto the mystery of Mary's
queenship. The description from the Book of Revelation of a great sign in the heavens, a woman clothed with the sun, the moon beneath her feet and a crown of twelve
stars on her head, is often understood, particularly in the liturgy, as an image of the
Virgin Mary, enthroned in heaven (Revelation 12:1). We see much of the same symbolism in the Virgin of Guadalupe. The heavenly sign, a symbol both of the church
and of Mary, presents the woman radiant in glory, majesty, and divine presence. This
vision is realized even now in Mary, and anticipated as the destiny of all the faithful.

Most importantly, the Gospel that Jesus himself preaches gives us insight into
Mary's queenship. The heart of Jesus' good news is the kingdom of God, already inaugurated in him, and powerfully displayed in his deeds of healing, forgiveness, and
compassion. Jesus' preaching in word and deed shows that God's kingdom is one of
humble service, welcome of the outcast, outpouring of love, and power to overcome
sin and evil. The first person to share fully in Jesus' establishment of God's reign is
his own mother. From her unwavering "yes" given to the angel Gabriel at the annunciation to her steadfast presence at the foot of the cross, Mary participated in Jesus'
work of making God's kingdom a dynamic reality. Her cooperation with her son in
showing forth the kingdom of God gives Mary a royal dignity even in the midst of
her humble human circumstances. After Jesus' death, she remained as a sign of God's
reign by praying faithfully with the disciples gathered in Jerusalem, and receiving the
Holy Spirit as part of the believing community.

God has promised that those who have died with Christ will also live with him, and those who remain faithful to the end will reign with him (II Timothy 2:11–12). Mary, ever-faithful maidservant of the Lord, is the first recipient of this sure promise. As she shared in extending God's reign throughout her life, Mary now shares in a heavenly rule. God's kingdom, no longer limited by time and space, is a universal and unending reign by which God unites all things in Christ, things in heaven and things on earth (Ephesians 1:10). Having raised her to eternal glory, God wills that Mary participate in this saving plan.

Mary's earthly and heavenly cooperation in actualizing God's reign reminds us that we, too, are commissioned through baptism to make the kingdom of God visible in our world. According to the Second Vatican Council, we are called to spread Christ's reign of truth and life, holiness and grace, justice, love, and peace (*Lumen Gentium* 36). In Mary we see the perfect model for our own participation in extending the kingdom of God. The Holy Father succinctly explains further significance of Mary's queenship for us:

> As the Queen who reigns in the glory of God's Kingdom, Mary remains close to us at every step of our earthly pilgrimage, supporting us in our trials and sharing with us the life and love of Jesus her Son.

Pope John Paul II,
General Audience,
Wednesday, 23 July 1997

FOR REFLECTION

What does "Mary remains close to us at every step of our earthly pilgrimage" mean to you? How have you experienced her?

How does contemplating Mary's queenship lead you to understand your own royal dignity?

The Fifth Glorious Mystery: The Coronation

The Fifth Glorious Mystery:
The Coronation

(STAND)

…your life is hidden with Christ in God.

(Colossians 3:3)

Our Father

(STAND)

I rejoice heartily in the LORD,
in my God is the joy of my soul;
For he has clothed me with a robe of salvation,
and wrapped me in a mantle of justice,
Like a bridegroom adorned with a diadem,
like a bride bedecked with her jewels.

(Isaiah 61:10)

Hail Mary (3)

A great sign appeared in the sky, a woman clothed with the sun,
with the moon beneath her feet, and on her head a crown of twelve stars.

(Revelation 12:1)

Hail Mary (3)

All glorious is the king's daughter as she enters,
her raiment threaded with gold;
In embroidered apparel she is led to the king.

(Psalm 45:14)

Hail Mary (3)

Blessed are you, daughter, by the Most High God…. Your deed of hope
will never be forgotten by those who tell of the might of God.

(Judith 13:18a, 19)

Hail Mary (1)

(STAND)

Glory to the Father

Concluding Dialogue and Prayer

(STAND)

SALVE REGINA
(Hail Mary)

Plainchant, Mode V

Sal - ve, Re - gí - na, ma - ter mi - se - ri - cór - di - ae: Vi - ta dul-
Hail, Ma - ry, moth - er and queen of ten - der mer - cy, our life, our

cé - do et spes no - stra, sal - ve. Ad te cla - má - mus,
com - fort, and our hope, we hail you. From this for - eign land

éx - su - les, fí - li - i He - vae. Ad te sus - pi - rá - mus,
Eve's sons and daugh - ters cry to you. So lost, so full of fear,

ge - mén - tes et flen - tes in hac la - cri - má - rum val - le.
we mourn, we grieve, we sigh from this tear - ful vale of ex - ile.

E - ia er - go, Ad - vo - cá - ta no - stra, il - los tu - os mi-
Ah, then, our help, our ad - vo - cate and guide, turn now to us the

se - ri - cór - des ó - cu - los ad nos con - vér - te.
gaze of your all - lov - ing eyes, so full of mer - cy.

Et Je - sum, be - ne - dí - ctum fruc - tum ven - tris tu - i,
And Je - sus — your Son, and Lord, your womb's most bless - ed fruit —

no - bis post hoc ex - sí - li - um os - tén - de.
show him to us when we com - plete our so - journ.

94

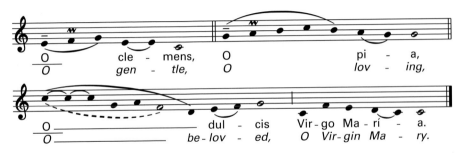

O	cle - mens,	O	pi - a,
O	gen - tle,	O	lov - ing,

O _____	dul - cis	Vir - go Ma - ri - a.
O _____	be - lov - ed,	O Vir - gin Ma - ry.

Latin text: Hermanus Contractus, 1013–1054, attr.
English text © 1995, Paul Ford. Published by OCP Publications. All rights reserved.

CLOSING DIALOGUE AND PRAYER

Bob Hurd

Priest/Leader

With you, Mary, may the church ever be - lieve

All

that God's word will be ful - filled.

Priest/Leader

With you, may the church ever say:

All

"Here am I, the servant of the Lord."

Priest/Leader

Pray for us, O Holy Mother of God,

All

that we may be made worthy of the promises of Christ.

Expansion of traditional text, based on Luke 1:38, 46 and music © 2003, Bob Hurd.
Published by OCP Publications. All rights reserved.

Priest/Leader: Let us pray:

O God, whose only begotten Son, by his life, death and resurrection,
has purchased for us the reward of eternal life;
grant, we beseech you, that by meditating on these mysteries of the most holy rosary
of the Blessed Virgin Mary, we may imitate what they contain and obtain what they
promise through Christ our Lord.

All: Amen.

SIGN OF THE CROSS

Bob Hurd

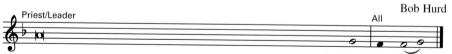

In the name of the Father, and of the Son, and of the Holy Spirit A-men.

LET IT BE DONE TO US

Bob Hurd

Verses

1, 5. Let it be done to us ac - cord - ing to your word.
2. And in the reign of God the hun - gry have their fill.
3. And in the reign of God the might - y be - come least.
4. In her own be - ing she be - came your dwell - ing place.

1, 5. Through us be spo - ken the Gos - pel to the world.
2. Let us break bread with all those who hun - ger still,
3. The poor are raised up to join the Prince of Peace.
4. And from her own flesh you took a hu - man face.

1, 5. Make us true dis - ci - ples with Mar - y who pro-claims:
2. trust - ing that God's prom - ise will one day be ful - filled:
3. Let our work for jus - tice pre - pare this ho - ly feast:
4. Make your church, like Mar - y, a sac - ra - ment of grace:

Refrain

Ma - gní - fi - cat, ma - gní - fi - cat, á - ni - ma me - a

Dó - mi - num, á - ni - ma me - a Dó - mi - num.

Bibliography & Resources on Mary & the Rosary

Print Resources

Baker, Robert J. and Barbara Budde, *A Sourcebook about Mary*. Chicago, IL:
  Liturgy Training Publications, 2002.

Brown, Donfried and Reumann Fitzmeyer, editors, *Mary in the New Testament*.
  Philadelphia: Fortress Press, 1978.

Cantalamessa, Raniero, OFM Cap, *Mary, Mirror of the Church*. Collegeville, MN:
  The Liturgical Press, 1992.

Crichton, J.D., *Our Lady in the Liturgy*. Collegeville, MN:
  The Liturgical Press, 1997.

Dubruiel, Michael, and Amy Welborn, *Praying the Rosary: With the Joyful,
  Luminous, Sorrowful, and Glorious Mysteries*. Huntington, IN:
  Our Sunday Visitor Publishing Division, 2003.

Graef, Hilda, *Mary, A History of Doctrine and Devotion*. Westminster:
  Christian Classics, 1965.

Hermes, Kathryn, *The Rosary: Contemplating the Face of Christ With Scripture
  and Icons*. Boston, MA: Pauline Books and Media, 2003.

LaVerdiere, Eugene, SSS, *The Annunciation to Mary: A Story of Faith, Luke 1:26–38*.
  Collegeville, MN: The Liturgical Press, 2004.

McKenna, Megan, *Praying the Rosary: A Complete Guide to the World's Most
  Popular Form of Prayer*. New York: Random House, 2004.

O'Carroll, CSSp, Michael, *Theotokos: A Theological Encyclopedia of the Blessed
  Virgin Mary*. Wilmington, DE: Michael Glazier, Inc., 1983.

Pelikan, Jaroslav, *Mary Through the Centuries*. New Haven and London:
  Yale University Press, 1996.

Rahner, Karl, *Mary, Mother of the Lord*. New York: Herder and Herder, 1963

Storey, William G., *Mother of the Americas: A Novena for Our Lady of Guadalupe*.
  Chicago, IL: Liturgy Training Publications, 2003.

Tavard, George H., *The Thousand Faces of the Virgin Mary*. Collegeville, MN:
  The Liturgical Press, 1996

United States Conference of Catholic Bishops, *A Rosary for Peace*.
  Washington, DC: USCCB Publishing, 2002.

United States Conference of Catholic Bishops, *A Scriptural Rosary for Justice and
  Peace*. Washington, DC: USCCB Publishing, 1998.

United States Conference of Catholic Bishops, *Book of Mary*. Washington, DC:
  USCCB Publishing, 1987.

United States Conference of Catholic Bishops, *Catechism of the Catholic Church,
  Second Edition*. New York: Doubleday Publishing, 2004.

United States Conference of Catholic Bishops, *Mary in the Church:
  A Compendium of Marian Documents*. Washington, DC: USCCB Publishing, 2003.

United States Conference of Catholic Bishops, *Unity and Diversity:
  A Scriptural Rosary*. Washington, DC: USCCB Publishing, 2001.

Church Documents on the Rosary

(listed chronologically and including Vatican internet site location)

Supremi Apostolatus Officio (The Supreme Apostolic Office),
Encyclical of Pope Leo XIII, on Devotion of the Rosary, September 1, 1883.
www.vatican.va/holy_father/leo_xiii/encyclicals/documents/hf_l-xiii_enc_
01091883_supremi-apostolatus-officio_en.html

Lumen Gentium (Dogmatic Constitution on the Church),
Pope Paul VI, November 21, 1964.
Chapter 8 (The Blessed Virgin Mary, Mother of God
in the Mystery of Christ and the Church).
www.vatican.va/archive/hist_councils/ii_vatican_council/documents/
vat-ii_const_19641121_lumen-gentium_en.html

Marialis Cultus (For the Right Ordering and Development of Devotion
to the Blessed Virgin Mary),
Apostolic Exhortation by Pope Paul VI, February 2, 1974.
www.vatican.va/holy_father/paul_vi/apost_exhortations/documents/hf_
p-vi_exh_19740202_marialis-cultus_en.html

Catechism of the Catholic Church, Articles 971, 2678, 2708; 1994,
updated September 1997.
www.vatican.va/archive/catechism/ccc_toc.htm

Direttorio Su Pietà Popolare e Liturgia (Directory on Popular Piety and the Liturgy),
Congregation for Divine Worship and the Discipline of the Sacraments, Principles
and Guidelines,
Chapter 5: Veneration of the Blessed Mother of Our Lord, The Rosary
(Sections 197–202), December 2001.
www.vatican.va/roman_curia/congregations/ccdds/documents/rc_con_ccdds_doc_
20020513_vers-direttorio_en.html

Rosarium Virginis Maria (The Rosary of the Blessed Virgin Mary),
Apostolic Letter by Pope John Paul II, October 16, 2002.
www.vatican.va/holy_father/john_paul_ii/apost_letters/documents/hf_
jp-ii_apl_20021016_rosarium-virginis-mariae_en.html